*This book is dedicated to all my guides
in physical and spirit form who
helped me understand and accept my abilities.*

About the Author

Anysia Kiel is a lifelong psychic medium and healer who has been able to perceive and communicate with spirits since she was a young child. Through her experiences in helping others, she has found that everyone holds the the ability to communicate with their own passed-on loved ones and friends. Anysia holds an MFA in creative writing and enjoys sharing information and exercises via her blog, Communicatingwithspirits, for people interested in learning more about mediumship development and healing. She is the founder of the Soul-Centered Healing Method, a system of healing that incorporates Divine light and which identifies and clears the spiritual and emotional root causes of illnesses, disease, trauma, and repetitive life patterns. Anysia created Soul-Centered Healing, a spiritual healing center in Toms River, NJ, through which she provides healing sessions, classes, lectures, and events. Visit her website at www.anysiakiel.com. Anysia lives in New Jersey with her husband and two children.

ANYSIA KIEL

Discovering
—— *the* ——
Medium
Within

TECHNIQUES & STORIES
FROM A PROFESSIONAL
PSYCHIC MEDIUM

Llewellyn Publications
Woodbury, Minnesota

FIRST EDITION
Third Printing, 2016

Book design by Bob Gaul
Cover art: Background © iStockphoto.com/rionm
            Picture frame © iStockphoto.com/Elemental Imaging
Cover design by Kevin Brown
Editing by Laura Graves

Llewellyn Publications is a registered trademark of Llewellyn Worldwide Ltd.

Library of Congress Cataloging-in-Publication Data (Pending)
978-0-7387-3667-9

Llewellyn Publications
A Division of Llewellyn Worldwide Ltd.
2143 Wooddale Drive
Woodbury, MN 55125-2989
www.llewellyn.com

Printed in the United States of America

Contents

Acknowledgments

Many people guided me along this magnificent journey. I thank God for my abilities with specific gratitude for the Holy Spirit, who gracefully guides me with wisdom and discernment in my work. I'm grateful to my parents for the generous, loving environment they provided and for fostering my connection with God. My siblings conveyed a balance of love and skepticism, which gave me the determination to push forward and seek purpose for my abilities. My husband, Shane, believed in me and always supported my connection to the spirit world; I'm grateful for his love and understanding. My children, Brayden and Briella, have been the biggest influences in my life. They've given me the greatest gift of unconditional love, which fueled my development of self-acceptance and true love. I thank my Aunt Jacquie, Uncle Dennis, and Aunt Jan for all of their love and understanding.

Several excellent English and writing professors inspired and enlightened me. From grammar and high school, I would like to thank Mrs. Susan Reynolds and the spirit of Ms. Sue Quinn, both of whom I credit with my initial engaging exposure to creative writing. From undergraduate college, I thank Dr. Michael Storey and Ms. Josephine Trueschler, for introducing literature as a passionate art form rather than mere words on a page. From graduate school, I thank my incredible thesis mentors Walter Cummins, Martin Donoff, and Jeffery Renard Allen. They nurtured the writer within me through grace and compassion without ever stifling my creative sense. I'm grateful for their collective patience, guidance, and support.

To my loved ones and friends in spirit form: your visits are always welcome as much as the insightful information you present; I leave the door open to all of you.

To John, Odessa, TK, SL, George, and RG—my spiritual entourage: I'm eternally grateful for your love and continued guidance.

To Kitty, Jay, Ricky, Nolanda, Jack, and Father Kevin: I appreciate your assistance in weaving the tapestry of our stories, which included Divine threads extending from the Earth plane to the spirit world.

To everyone who has ever visited my office: thank you for trusting and allowing me to work in the sacred space of your energy.

I gratefully acknowledge my editor, Amy Glaser, for her keen vision and intuitive understanding of this book. She recognized the book's ability to help people and decided to pursue it. I also thank my publisher Llewellyn Worldwide for supporting me as an author and rising to the task of publishing books, which elevate human consciousness.

Introduction

As a young child, seeing spirits scared me. As my clairaudience developed, however, I learned to communicate with them. My first conversations involved passed-on loved ones. I felt quite comfortable with their visits, and using my childhood rationale, I decided that I must have been chosen as the universal family member. Since our family members in spirit form conveyed validating details for those on the Earth plane, most of my immediate family learned to accept these visits and messages.

When I grew older, I became more sensitive to energy; I saw, sensed, and heard spirits everywhere, although it didn't quite meld with my Catholic upbringing. It became normal for me and I soon recognized that my concept of "normal" was different from that of most other people. I hid my abilities from my friends and non-family members out of fear of being judged and rejected.

All of that changed when a good friend from work passed on and opened me to communicating with non-family members. He had many messages for his loved ones, friends, and coworkers, and his visits pushed me along the path of mediumship. People in my company eventually learned of my abilities, and I received requests for mediumship readings in voicemails, emails, and sometimes on notes during company meetings. Although it was not something I was doing as a professional psychic medium, I felt bad saying no because they wanted to communicate with a loved one, and I had a God-given ability to facilitate that process. I never rejected a request, and it helped me grow in my abilities.

Non-family members and strangers in spirit form began showing up regularly. They often had a connection to someone I knew or someone my family members knew. Despite my fears and misgivings, I felt I had a responsibility to help those who visited me. This self-imposed level of obligation catalyzed my initial acceptance. The fact that I could see, feel, smell, and hear them when others couldn't meant that I needed to help them. I knew God gave me these abilities for a reason, and I needed to find it.

I decided to embrace my skills when I first realized my son had the abilities to see and communicate with spirits at the age of two. I felt happy to have a child just like me. He had psychic, mediumistic, and remote viewing abilities. Shortly after, my daughter was born with mediumistic skills. She could identify relatives in photos who had passed on long before her birth. She saw them in the house and communicated with them often. I knew my children had the abilities for specific purposes, and I vowed to guide them in their processes of learning and utilizing their abilities. My children helped me shed my fears, and I began to spread my wings in the realm of mediumship.

Around the same time I recognized my daughter's abilities, I began sensing energy with my palms. It seemed like I had tiny wheels in my hands that often became heated. If I put my palms against my body, they exuded a warm, soothing energy.

I soon found a purpose for this energy coming out my hands. One of our dogs had a torn ligament in his knee and needed surgery. We scheduled the surgery with an orthopedic surgeon for a date four weeks out. Every night, I placed my hands on his knee for a few minutes as the warm energy radiated through me, out my hands, and into his body. The day of the surgery, the orthopedic surgeon made the dog walk down the hall, and amazingly, the dog's gait was perfect. The doctor would not operate on the dog because the ligament had miraculously healed.

A wonderful cousin of mine (there are several psychics and healers on my father's side) was teaching a Reiki I class, and I enrolled. Reiki gave me the basics of energy healing, an understanding of auras, chakras, and how energy is conducted through the body. It was a perfect complement to my psychic and mediumship skills.

As I conducted healing sessions on family and friends, in a bedroom in my house, I learned to incorporate my psychic and mediumistic skills into healing work. When I gently waved my hands over peoples' bodies, I could see, feel, and hear all the experiences they had stored in their energies. If someone had been abused or experienced any type of trauma, I could see it. I could hear their unspoken thought patterns. If they had fears, I could feel them and know what they were about. If there was an illness, I would ask about the root of the disease and I would get an answer. As a psychic, I could perceive everything in their energy fields.

In addition, if someone in spirit form needed to come through to help the person on earth heal; the spirit would present itself during the healing session and convey pertinent information. Oftentimes, multiple family members in spirit form would present themselves during a healing session. Sometimes it would seem like a family reunion, as if the passed-on relatives seized the opportunity to connect with their living family member. The experiences demonstrated how mediumship is a tangible tool for healing.

I never really thought I would work as a professional psychic medium, but it evolved that way for me. I had a small shared office in a nursing facility close to my home. I only worked a few times a month, dipping my toes in the pool of this sort of work.

The space worked well, but I eventually needed a dedicated space of my own. I found a small office in the center of town and opened Soul-Centered Healing. As I accepted my abilities, I also accepted myself; the two were intertwined. The journey of self and acceptance as a psychic medium has been lifelong and adventurous, to say the least. The more I embraced my abilities, the more comfortable I felt in my own skin. Having two children with the same abilities also prodded me on my path. I didn't want them to feel like it was wrong to be themselves—the way I felt most of my life—so I nurtured them in their abilities.

I hold the belief that everyone has potential psychic and mediumistic abilities. Our abilities lie dormant in our souls until we choose to engage them. When we shed our fears like butterflies emerging from chrysalises, we open ourselves to the magnificent energetic world around us. As we spread our wings and embrace our abilities, we can fly through the world peacefully, enjoying life's sweet nectar.

I've included exercises in this book for psychic and mediumistic skill development. They're basic and don't require anything but an open mind. I hope all readers of this book try these exercises. Through thought, we can transcend space, and as you master these exercises, you will find that your loves ones are only a thought away. They've changed form from physical to spiritual and they open the door to a new everlasting spiritual relationship with you. Let the journey begin!

ONE

The Visitors

As a child, I always slept with a blanket over my head so I couldn't see them. They usually came at night, or when I took a nap. I felt them standing next to my bed—silently watching, waiting. My body filled with a strange vibrating heat, and a high-pitched buzzing noise rang through my ears whenever they came. I thought they wanted to tell me something, but they remained silent. I wondered why they never showed up at the dinner table, in school, or at a store—why only when I was alone?

For years I tried to tell my mother about these experiences, but she didn't believe me, dismissing what I said. I received a worse reaction from my father.

"There's no one in your room. Stop telling tall tales," he said. He always became angry and hollered when I told him about the visitors. By the age of nine, I gave up trying to convince my parents, realizing they couldn't see what I saw, heard, or felt. My experiences were strange; I was different from other people. I felt vulnerable and isolated, like a single leaf left on a barren tree before the first frost.

Sometimes I cried under my blanket when they came, powerless and immobilized by the sight of them. I never knew any of them, so I wasn't sure how they found me. But they wanted something and waited intently for it every time. I stayed under the blanket, eyes closed, chanting with heated breath, "Please go away. Please go away." I knew they left when the buzzing stopped in my ears and the vibrating heat dissipated. Once they were gone, I removed the blanket that covered my head and shielded my eyes from seeing them. I had so many questions but no one to ask. What did they want? Why me? Did they show up in all kids' rooms? My brother and sister never mentioned seeing them. Why did God let them come to me?

My mother and father said I had a blanket as long as they could remember. I cried often as an infant, and the only thing that comforted me was a blanket over my head. According to my parents, on a hot summer day at the beach, when I was two years old, I screamed for over thirty minutes. My loud cries attracted the attention of many beachgoers who gaped and gawked at my parents. My mother tried giving me toys, food, a drink, picking me up, changing my diaper, but nothing soothed the cries. According to my mother, she gave me my blanket and as I placed it over my head, the crying ceased. She said a woman on a neighboring blanket warned my mother that I could over-heat with the blanket over my head. The woman asked my mother if she could take it off my head. Apparently, my mother told the woman to mind her own business, and once I fell asleep, my parents took the blanket off my head.

As I grew older, a blanket over my head became nor-mal for me. Nanny, my maternal grandmother, quilted me a small blanket I used every night. My family teased me about being a big baby needing my "blankie" to sleep at night. They didn't believe what I saw in my room and would never have believed that I used the blanket to hide. I gave up explaining and trying to defend myself, resign-ing to the mockery for years.

We had a cemetery at the top of our block—yes, a small family cemetery in the middle of a residential de-velopment. It sounds strange, right? What I find even stranger is that my parents chose to live on that particular street, when they had a choice of that same model house on four other streets. When I asked my parents why they chose the street with a cemetery on it, my mother said that she thought it was an interesting feature. I reminded her that features are usually what one considers an asset more like well-landscaped yards, fancy street lights, tree-lined roads, or a neighboring play area. Somehow a plot of land filled with dead bodies didn't strike me as an "asset" in a residential development. My father said he never even gave it a second thought. His response didn't surprise me; he had a knack for blocking out things that made him uncomfortable, especially my stuff. I think it was a kind of coping mechanism. He worked as a deputy fire chief in Newark, New Jersey. He had witnessed all types of injuries and deaths. Maybe blocking out those memories, images, and experiences helped him do his job.

The Rodgers family owned the cemetery. Their house was the very first one at the top of the block, right in front of the cemetery. At one time, the family owned most of the land in our area. Eventually, it was sold to a developer who built homes on it. A chain-link fence bordered the cemetery, the latter of which housed rows of small white marble headstones with family names etched on their fronts. I didn't really pay too much attention to it until I was about ten or eleven years old. At that age, my mom sent me to the grocery store up the block on a regular basis. Whenever I walked up to the A & P to buy whatever my mom needed, I purposely raised my hand to the side of my face so I wouldn't see anything as I passed the cemetery.

Eventually, I felt the "visitors" around me more often, inside and outside my home, but only when I was alone. I sensed them in all rooms in my house, in my yard, walking home from the bus stop, riding my bike, and on the swings at the playground. I could perceive them hovering around me, invading my energy. The warm sensation they exuded grew hotter as they drew closer to me.

"I don't want to see you," I called out. They didn't show themselves, but I still felt them there staring intently as my body temperature rose. Sometimes I could see a silhouette or a strange break in the flow of energy—vibrating lines that formed an outline of a body. I think they respected my wishes to not see them physically, but I couldn't make them go away completely. I still felt them everywhere.

I sensed them more in crowds, and I would get overwhelmed in crowded areas. I'm not sure if it was because there were so many of them in a confined space or if it was from the heat they gave off. I remember this happening when we went to densely populated malls or when we visited cities. I would be walking and all of the sudden, a heated feeling overwhelmed my whole body like someone had cast me out into a barren desert in the heat of the day, leaving me there. It sapped my strength, and I'd have to sit down for a few minutes until it passed. It made me fear going into crowded areas.

One time, my family visited the World Trade Center in Manhattan and we needed to take an underground railway called the PATH to get there. When we got on the PATH at the Newark terminal, it was filled with people. My mother and brother sat across from me, and I sat down between two strangers. My dad stood along with a host of others in the center of the train, gripping hand straps from the ceiling for support.

As the doors closed and we proceeded down the tunnel, I felt the heat building in my body. I sensed *them* all around. It seemed like everyone on the train had a few with them but didn't know it. I grew weaker and felt myself getting dizzy. By the second stop, I didn't think I would make it, and my ears started buzzing.

"I think I'm gonna pass out," I said to my mother, as I felt myself sweating. She peered through the line of people standing in the center. She gave me a smile and reminded me that the ride was only twenty minutes.

"If you freak out and embarrass us, I swear I'll punch you in your face," my brother Terence said. I admired him for his deep sense of compassion. He had the makings of a Dalai Lama. Actually, if he had responded differently, I would've thought he was sick or maybe hit his head. At least his behavior was consistent; he never understood and couldn't relate.

"It's only another few minutes, honey. Just hang on. Everything's fine," my mother said. I leaned back and rested my head on the seat. I kept telling myself that everything was fine but I also kept saying in my mind, "Please stay away. It's not a good time." We pulled into the World Trade Center and once again there were more crowds. The line for the elevator to the observation deck in tower two coiled around the lobby like a serpent. We snaked through the lobby in that line for just under an hour.

They packed us like sardines in the elevator and finally took us to the top. When we stepped out, I felt like I could breath again. We had glass-enclosed views from 107 stories above the city. We took a small escalator up to the 110th floor and stepped out into the clear, unobstructed, open-air sights over 1,000 feet above New York City. The heat and weak feelings drifted away in the soft rippling breeze. The city looked so small and manageable from that height. Yellow taxis seemed like children's toys moving along the small roadways. I could see for miles as we walked along the roof and savored the 360-degree view.

We took a ferry ride to Ellis Island next. I enjoyed the boat ride because we sat up top and watched the sights drift by as the cool air rolled over us. Most people stayed inside on the lower level, so we didn't have any crowding. About half the people exited the boat for Ellis Island, while the others continued on to visit the Statue of Liberty.

When we got off the boat, we walked around and took pictures. My father searched for his grandparents' names on the American Immigrant Wall of Honor outside the building. There were rows and rows of etched names of people who left their homelands to make new lives for their families. It was amazing to see how many people had the courage to leave everything in the hopes of creating a better life. I wondered if those people felt scared when they boarded the boats for the long voyage to the United States. Most of them didn't know anyone besides their families, had very little money, and had to find work as soon as they got here. I was filled with a deep sense of respect and admiration for each and every person as I walked past those names.

When we stepped through the doors of the large brick building, we entered an open room lined with white tiles. I walked around in the room and could feel how busy it had once been. Images of the people who had walked through that room flooded my mind. There were millions of them, although I had no idea how I was able to see and feel these things. We proceeded through the museum, where they had set up various stations with recorded information and original artifacts like baggage, clothing, and other items used during that time. As we were funneled in and out of the rooms, I felt some heaviness in the space.

We entered a quarantine area and I felt overwhelmed with sadness. If someone had a communicable illness or disease, they were relegated to a quarantine area, where medical staff evaluated and cared for them. According to the recording at the museum, the people in quarantine were kept there to minimize the spreading illnesses. I detected some of them as I moved through the rooms of the museum. They hovered in the form of a warm physical sensation. It seemed like they followed me through the rooms, waiting for something from me. My ears buzzed intensely and I just kept saying in my mind, "I don't want to see you. Please go away."

It wasn't until my paternal grandmother died that I actually understood what they wanted from me. Grandma, affectionately known by all her grandchildren as "Gram," was diagnosed with an aggressive form of lung cancer. Her disease spread rapidly and had advanced to her brain. Gram told my aunt that she wanted to fight it. She agreed to try chemotherapy but it was unsuccessful. She died within six weeks of her initial diagnosis.

On her last day on Earth, the hospital staff summoned us to her bedside to say our final goodbyes. My father, uncle, and aunt—her three children—were already there. My cousins, my sister, my brother, and I filed into the drab beige room and encircled her bed. A smothering, dense energy filled the room and bore down on us, as if there wasn't enough air to breathe. I'm not sure if it was the energy of impending death or deep grief. I felt like I needed to leave the room, as I breathed deeply with little relief from the pressure. It seemed like most of the oxygen had been sucked out of the room.

Gram looked thin and frail with all the tubes stuck in her arms. Her translucent yellow skin matched the yellowing in her eyes—a physical sign that cancer had defeated her liver. A pink silk cap covered her balding head. My father caressed her hand and told her that it was okay to go. She glanced over at him. She couldn't talk, but breathed quick, short breaths. It seemed like she was fighting to stay in her body but someone was pulling her away like a game of tug-of-war.

I remember my sister, brother, and I went to the cafeteria with our cousins to get a soda. Seated at a round table with our cups, we talked about happy memories with Gram. We told funny stories that elicited deep belly laughs and warm smiles that lit up the gray-walled cafeteria. As soon as we stepped through the doorway to Gram's room, she took her last breath. The place fell silent and for a moment; it seemed like we froze in time. I didn't say a word. I didn't think anything would come out even if I tried. But I still felt her there, next to me. My body held the warm vibration, yet my ears didn't buzz. I heard her say, "I love you." Then a gentle breeze brushed my left shoulder; I knew she was gone. My father went around the room and hugged and kissed everyone in the tear-filled place, as I studied the empty body propped up like a puppet in the hospital bed. I wondered where she had gone and how I heard her voice after she left her body behind. I never spoke of the incident.

One of my grandmother's ongoing requests while alive was to have me sing and record "Let There Be Peace on Earth" so she could play it whenever she wanted. She asked multiple times over the last couple of years before her death and I guess I thought she'd always be around, so I put off fulfilling her request. When it came time to plan the funeral, my dad and his siblings had to choose the music.

"'Let There Be Peace on Earth' was mom's favorite," my father said. "That one has to be in the mass." A guilt-filled pang pierced my heart.

"You could sing that song, Anysia," my aunt said. "She always loved hearing you sing." I agreed to do it because I knew I should have done it when she was alive. I had no idea how I would pull it off, though, since I hadn't sung in at least five years.

On the morning of the funeral, I tried warming up my voice by practicing some a capella scales in my bedroom. My voice cracked and sounded weak. *I can't do this*, I thought to myself. I walked toward the door, and just then, the air conditioner in the room turned itself on. I walked over and inspected the dial. My body warmed as a vibrating energy penetrated my chest and my heart raced a bit.

"Yes you can," I heard Gram say. I ran to my mother's room and told her what happened and for once, she actually believed me. I'm not sure if it was the physical tangibility of something turning on in her own home that convinced her or the fact that it involved someone close to her that passed. Either way, joy enveloped me as I finally got someone in my family on board.

I knew Gram was there next to me as the first few notes echoed from the loud pipe organ in the choir loft. An overwhelming impression of love and warmth blanketed my body—I couldn't contain the flowing sensation of loving comfort, and tears slid down my cheeks. Gazing downward, I noticed the casket adorned in a cloak of deep red roses being carried by the pallbearers: my dad, uncle, and male cousins. My relatives filed neatly from pews to the center aisle and out the church. I sang the song as loving images of my Gram and my childhood flashed through my mind like a sentimental silent film. When I finished singing, I wiped my tear-drenched cheeks with tissues and descended the choir loft stairs. The funeral procession continued out the doors, but my aunt and mother greeted me with hugs. I still sensed Gram's warm, loving presence. I heard her whisper, "thank you" in my right ear, and I wasn't scared.

I experienced the deep sadness of parental loss through my father, aunt, and uncle during that time. They were devastated adult orphans left with only memories and material things. If I had the foreknowledge to understand that sharing my communication with my Gram could have helped them heal, I would have told them what I saw, felt, and heard. But in retrospect, I think I kept it from them out of fear of being ridiculed. My aunt might have believed me, but I knew my father and uncle wouldn't take that leap of faith.

After Gram's funeral, many discarnate relatives visited with messages for our living family members. They were always easily recognizable, so I was never afraid. They showed themselves in familiar clothes or with a particular hairstyle and looked the way they did right before they passed. They brought familiar scents such as perfumes or candy, rousing deep, nostalgic feelings in me, and giving me specific validating information for each recipient.

I often wrote the information down so I wouldn't forget it. These bittersweet visits carried mixed emotions: there was happiness for the connection I still had with them, but sadness because I couldn't reach out and give them hugs or kisses. I enjoyed the feelings of loving comfort they brought with them. Their energies provided peace and safety for me because they could protect me from other non-family spirits, or at least I believed they could.

TWO

New Homes and the Spirits in Them

I left for college that summer with a bit of anxiety. I attended an all-female school in Baltimore and didn't know a soul. It wasn't my first choice, but that school gave me a talent scholarship and college work-study, so it was the best financial fit for my family. It was also within the two-hour drive limit my parents had set for me. I wasn't allowed to apply to any schools that were more than a two-hour drive from my home, in case I got sick or had some other emergency that necessitated my parents driving to get me. I rendered the rule obsolete after my first year because I either took the train home, got a ride from a friend, or my grandparents drove me home.

I had always dreamed of attending one of those big coed schools with an enormous college band that played at all the games for the magnificent conference-winning championship football team, but it wasn't in the cards for me. In my junior year of high school, I envisioned myself in amphitheater classrooms with hundreds of seats filled with a myriad of students from diverse backgrounds. I really enjoyed the thought of being a small fish in a big pond. But instead, I was a bigger fish in a smaller pond.

The beautiful campus was built in a parklike setting with lots of green grass along tree-lined paths, though it was steps away from downtown Baltimore. It only had two dorms: one freshman/sophomore, and one junior/senior. Many of the students commuted from instate, something I didn't know when I applied to the school.

The only initial advantage was that my maternal grandparents lived in Arlington, Virginia—just an hour's drive away. I was excited about spending time with my grandparents. They had always lived in Virginia, and I only got to see them a few times a year. Going to school in Baltimore afforded us the opportunity to catch up on lost time.

I made acquaintances quickly because the school's thorough freshman orientation program orchestrated lots of bonding, engaging activities to facilitate the transition from home to dorm living. I met lots of nice girls, most of whom lived in Maryland. We spent many hours meeting new faces and learning names and by the time the semester began, I knew many people and felt right at home.

Ironically, I soon found out that this school was very much like my home. Part of the school's campus butted up against an old cemetery, a fact I discovered by accident. I walked down Homeland Avenue because it was a short cut to the Rite Aid on York Road. Stunning brick homes with sprawling green yards and colorful flowers lined the left side of the street. On the right side of the street was a large cemetery that dated back to the 1800s. The white marble and limestone headstones and plot markers varied in style and shape—large angels and crosses, pyramids, oversized urns, and upright squares.

Initially, I made the trek a few times with friends to buy nail polish and other toiletry items. The first time we walked past the cemetery, I noticed a woman darting in and out of the larger headstones. She moved quickly, so I only glimpsed her as I continued conversing with the girls. The female spirit startled me because I hadn't seen an unknown (non-family member) spirit since childhood. I wondered why I could see her. She wore a long, dark dress. I couldn't tell if it was a deep green or black. It was long sleeved with a high collar covering her neck. Her hair was pulled back in a sort of bun—I couldn't tell exactly what type of bun or twist because I only viewed her from the front. Our eyes met and I looked away.

I didn't say anything about the female spirit to the other girls I was with; I didn't want to scare them, and

I didn't want them to think I was crazy. If they could've seen her, I thought, they would've pointed her out. I pretended not to see her. I had enough on my plate, adjusting to my new environment. I needed to blend in like a chameleon. My primary focuses were to get good grades, make friends, and experience college…not necessarily in that order. Dealing with spirits in Baltimore was not on the top of my list of things to do at school. Actually, it wasn't even on the bottom of my list. I think I had it on the list of things *not* to do!

As time went on, I grew more comfortable walking by the cemetery on my own. It felt peaceful, like an extension of the campus. When I saw the woman peering from behind a headstone, I would smile at her, look away, and keep right on walking. She never said anything or approached me, nor did I speak to or approach her. We had a sort of sense of respectful distance between us, like a little secret. I wasn't scared of her because she didn't bother me or seem to want anything from me. I actually thought she watched over me on my walks, and it made me feel safe.

Even though the school in Baltimore wasn't my first choice, I grew to love it. I studied liberal arts with emphases in English and philosophy. I had excellent professors in both disciplines and learned a lot academically and personally. I really evolved into an independent person with my own thoughts, opinions, and preferences. I didn't miss the influence of my family or my friends.

I also fell in love with the city, which intoxicated me with all its hidden treasures. I visually enjoyed the old brownstones and red brick rowhouses with their colorful displays of painted screens brightening the city. The cobblestone streets held the energy of carriage horses and buggies long before they bore the treads of tires. The old downtown buildings quietly conveyed deep history waiting to be explored. I felt at home in that city. There was so much to do, and everything was accessible. I loved the restaurants in Federal Hill, the Oriole games at Memorial Stadium and later at Camden Yards, concerts at Peabody Conservatory, architecture in Mount Vernon, the local bars in Fells Point, and the shops of the Gallery and Inner Harbor. The sights, sounds, and experiences of Baltimore created a new home for me, and I felt like I belonged there.

My second *new home* was in Arlington, Virginia. My grandparents picked me up twice a month during the four years at school, and I spent weekends at their home. Sometimes we visited the sites of Washington, D. C., but most times Nanny and I went shopping and enjoyed each other's company. We gave each other manicures, pedicures, and makeovers with Mary Kay clay facial masks and makeup. She always let me style her hair all different ways, though her short gray hair limited our styling choices. During my senior year, we tried many different hairstyles, searching for the best fit to style our hair for my upcoming wedding to my high school sweetheart, Shane. Occasionally, I brought a friend with me, and Nanny cooked delicious Italian specialties like eggplant parmigiana and chicken cutlets with broccoli rabe. She stocked the house with all my favorites snacks and homemade treats.

Whenever I visited Nanny and Pops's colonial-style home as a child, I always stayed in the small bedroom that housed Nanny's craft supplies and other spare items. Since my parents weren't there when I visited during college, I stayed in the large bedroom that had been reserved for my mom and dad during family visits.

On my first visit, I brought a bunch of clothes with me. I unpacked and placed them in the drawers. I had some items to hang in the closet, but as I grabbed the black iron latch to open the door, a feeling of dread filled my body, like I was going to see something horrific when I opened it. I took a deep breath and pulled the door back slowly, but I only saw two empty racks with a few wooden hangers. I detected a male energy that was both depressive and heavy. I also experienced a pressure in my throat. I hung up my two dresses and quickly closed the door.

That night at dinner, I asked my grandparents if they were the first owners of the house. They said it had been built in 1941, and they bought it in 1971 from an older couple who lived there, the Stevensons. I knew something had happened in that upstairs closet, but I didn't press the issue. My grandparents didn't mention anything, and I didn't want to worry or scare them. But during the rest of that visit, the closet door kept opening by itself. It creaked eerily as it slowly opened each time. Eventually, I pushed my suitcase in front of it to keep it shut.

Pops usually worked on Saturdays, so Nanny and I often spent the day doing special things. She taught me how to cook, sew, and do laundry. Nanny loved herbs and flowers; she made her own perfume, potpourri, and handmade oils and creams. She grew many herbs and flowers in yard. In the spring, her yard lit up with brightly colored tulips, bearded irises, and sunny yellow daffodils, or jonquils, as Pops called them. Rainbows of flowers lined the perimeter of the yard and colored the front walkway to the white brick house.

The neighbor across the street, Tom, had a giant magnolia tree. As Pops was a Louisiana transplant, the scent of blooming magnolias reminded him of home. Every time I came for a visit, Nanny had fresh white magnolia blossoms the size of my hand arranged in a vase on the dining room table. The lemony magnolia scent pervaded the rooms of the house and reminded me of warm sunny weather.

The back room on the first floor doubled as a greenhouse. It had a double-hung bay window with a large copper table against it filled with green houseplants. Nanny watered them each day and spritzed the leaves. She spent a great deal of time in that room because of the natural light, and also I think the energy of the plants comforted her. We always ate our breakfast there and had our afternoon tea in that room, in front of all the plants. I loved learning new things from Nanny, but most of all I loved spending time with her, especially in her beautiful yard among her color-ful gardens or in the back room filled with her lively plants.

Nanny had a knack for nature—an invariable green thumb—and a deep connection to the earth. She intro-duced me to essential oils for medicinal purposes. I could pick up a plant in any garden center, and she could identify it and relay its medicinal attributes. She revered lavender oil for its varied uses and always had a small amber bottle of it in the house. She never attended college, but her knowledge of plants, herbs, and nature seemed strangely innate. I don't know where or how she acquired all that knowledge, but she readily shared it with me.

On another visit to the house, I unpacked my things and opened the closet to hang my dress. Cowering in the back corner, I noticed the side view of a thin, middle-aged man. He sat on the floor with his arms wrapped around his knees. He wore a uniform of some sort. It was a dark green shirt and pants. He also had a matching hat. He didn't say a word. He glanced over at me and then put out his head down again. I got the distinct feeling he had committed suicide in that closet. A moment later, he dis-appeared. I never saw him again.

I remember as a child, my sister hated that closet be-cause she felt scared of it. The door always opened by itself and the light turned on. My father also confessed that he could never get a good night's sleep in that room because he always felt like someone was watching him. Meanwhile, my mother snored loudly every time we slept there, apparently unaffected by the room's energy. Obviously, the psychic abilities in our family are stronger on my dad's side!

After I saw the man the closet, I never slept in that room again during my college years. I told Nanny the queen-sized bed was too big for me, and I needed something smaller. I had to walk through my grandparents' room to get to the smaller bedroom (it had a twin bed) but I didn't mind—at least it was spirit-free.

As I wrote this chapter, I relayed this story to my Uncle Dennis, my mother's brother. He said that the previous owners of Nanny and Pops's house told them someone had died in that bedroom. According to my uncle, the Stevensons were the second owners of the house. My uncle said that the Stevensons told Nanny and Pops that the first owners of the house had a son who shot himself in that room, which had been his bedroom. My uncle didn't know if the death occurred specifically in that closet, but he knew it happened in that room. I guess I could have told Nanny and Pops what I felt because they already knew about it. Apparently, like my mother, they were unaffected by the energy in the house. This information once again affirms that there were limited psychic abilities on my maternal side.

Toward the end of my senior year in college, Nanny had a massive stroke, which rendered her unable to speak or move, though she was completely lucid. She could only utter indiscernible sounds and grunts. Pops didn't want to put her in a nursing home, so he transformed into her full-time nurse and caretaker, feeding her baby food and bathing her daily. It was strange seeing him as the nurturer. He came off like a tough guy with his six-foot-three-inch robust build. He reminded me of a retired pro wrestler. Whenever we visited, it pained me to see her lying there as she did, trapped in the broken shell that was her body. The only consolation was that Pops had her hospital bed set in her favorite room of the house. Her bed replaced the plant-filled table against the window. I knew she loved that room and enjoyed the natural light. She could see the birds flying to the many feeders, and she could feel the sun on her face. When I visited, I talked to her while I watered her plants and spritzed all the leaves for her. I assured her that they were all healthy and thriving.

On my wedding day, June 11, 1994, I called Nanny and told her I loved her and wished she could be with me. She mumbled some sounds I couldn't understand. But I felt her deep sadness in my heart and tears filled my eyes. During the wedding, we placed flowers on the altar for those family members who couldn't be with us for the ceremony. I thought of Nanny as I set the roses down and sent her loving thoughts. When I heard the first few notes of "Ave Maria" from the pipe organ, tears welled in my eyes. As the cantor sung the Franz Schubert version, Nanny's favorite, I lowered my head and sobbed. I actually got makeup all over my gloves wiping my tears away. I definitely missed Nanny that day; the wedding was not as joyful without her presence.

My husband and I were supposed to fly out to Saint Lucia bright and early the next morning for a beautiful ten-day honeymoon, courtesy of my in-laws. I believe we had a 6:00 am flight. But as we boarded the plane, something felt really wrong. I told Shane we couldn't take the trip, and he looked over at me and said that I was probably just tired. I was tired because we had gone to bed in the early hours of the morning, but the impression I had was more than exhaustion. I had a horrible feeling of despair in my gut and I grabbed my bag from the overhead compartment and walked off the plane.

"Are you nuts?" Shane asked as he gritted his teeth in the middle of the terminal. I cried because I didn't know why I had that feeling, but I knew I shouldn't take the trip. We decided to stay with my parents for the next week until we left for Idaho. Shane had to return to the Air Force base out there. Initially we had planned on driving to Idaho the day after we got back from the honeymoon, but our plans had changed. Instead of basking together on a warm island beach, for the next ten days we were sleeping in my parents' house on my twin bed from childhood, which wasn't even remotely romantic or comfortable! Plus, even though I was married, I felt like a child again in my parents' home.

Five days after my wedding, a ringing telephone pierced the nighttime silence at two in the morning. My heart beat quickly as I anticipated the bad news. My grandfather's neighbor, Rae, said that my Nanny had died. Pops was talking to the police and paramedics and couldn't come to the phone. I remember hearing those words and feeling a part of me slip into darkness, as I quietly passed the phone to my mother. Suddenly the happy memories of my time with Nanny were erased. The only image I could recall was the one of her lying helpless in the hospital bed at her house. I lost my Nanny that day; a person who mothered and loved me, and most of all, a dear friend. A few moments later, my mother sobbed uncontrollably, and I patted her back, trying to ease her sadness. She laid on her side in the spare bedroom and struggled for little breaths between sobs. I stroked her short brown hair and told her that it would be okay. I knew how she felt because I sensed it too—total loss and complete sadness like someone took an eraser and wiped away a favorite person in my life forever.

If we had taken that honeymoon, we would have missed Nanny's funeral. I had promised Nanny that I would sing "Ave Maria" at her funeral. Ironically after I sang at Gram's funeral a few years earlier, Nanny asked me to sing at hers too.

"I just thought that was lovely," Nanny said. "I want you to sing at mine someday, except I want you to sing 'Ave Maria'," she stated. She loved the song for two reasons: She was a second-generation Italian American, and her first name was Maria. It seemed like an odd request because she wasn't even close to being sick at the time, but I nodded my head and promised I'd do it. If I missed the funeral, I would've broken my promise. I'd almost broken a promise to Gram but pulled out just fine in the end. I needed to do the same for Nanny. Somehow, psychically, I was able to perceive Nanny's passing before it happened.

I didn't usually tune into precognitive information unless someone in spirit facilitated the process. I believe someone in spirit let me know I shouldn't take that trip for a very important reason.

Shane got over his anger at missing the honeymoon. My mother-in-law was able to get an exchange for the plane tickets and the timeshare, so my in-laws took the trip as a vacation a year later. Shane didn't understand it all, but agreed that there had to be other nonphysical forces at work with the cancellation of the trip and timing of Nanny's death making them more than coincidental. I was happy he understood and grateful for his openness to the energy and my abilities, since he had not yet experienced them fully. He knew that I saw and felt spirits, and he knew about the incident with Gram's passing. I had not fully explained everything to him, since I didn't quite understand it myself. I had hoped the situation would unveil itself in a timely yet slow enough pace so he wouldn't be overwhelmed by all of it.

THREE

The Family Messenger

After Nanny died, many strange things happened. Shane and I had an alarm clock in our apartment bedroom that kept going off at all hours, though we never set it. We replaced the clock three times, and all the replacements did the same thing. Our lease was up on our apartment, so we moved in with my in-laws for two months while our builder finished our house. One night, as we all slept soundly, the alarm clock blared at 3:00 am in our room, waking everyone. The alarm wasn't set and my mother-in-law inspected it carefully. The clock had been in the bedroom for over ten years and this had never happened before. Everyone went back to sleep, but I stayed awake and pondered the possibility that someone might be trying to get our attention.

The same thing happened with the alarm clock when we moved into our brand-new house. Also, all of the smoke alarms in our house, which were not hard-wired, blared at odd hours without a sign of smoke or fire. They stopped when we removed the batteries. As with the alarm clocks, we replaced them, but the new ones kept going off just like their predecessors. We knew something strange was going on, but we weren't sure who or what was to blame.

We went down to Arlington, Virginia to visit Pops. It was our first time at the house, since Nanny had passed. Every year, I visited Pops and Nanny the third week of October and took a day trip down to the Saint Mary's County Oyster Festival. We began the tradition my freshman year in college with Nanny and kept it up even though we substituted a teammate—Shane for Nanny. Shane and I arrived in Arlington on a Friday night and spent all day Saturday at the festival. That year, we brought our new puppy, a four-month-old chocolate Labrador retriever named Timber. Pops loved Timber's company. We sat in the yard Friday night and grilled out while Pops threw a tennis ball to Timber until his little brown legs couldn't run any longer.

I felt very sad being at the house without Nanny. The house energy felt quiet and lifeless. I figured Pops spent most of his time at work to minimize the loneliness at home. Pops had cleared the plants off the table in the back room and replaced it in front of the large window. I ventured into the room as I returned from the bathroom. When I stood in front of the window without all the lively plants, I recalled all the mornings Nanny and I ate breakfast or had afternoon tea in front of that window. I missed those times and cried a bit by myself, wishing she could be there again with me.

The next day we drove to the festival and had a blast. They had oysters prepared in every way possible. They also had all kinds of other foods like seafood and barbeque. I always got fried oysters and steamed shrimp. Shane got oysters sometimes on the half-shell, while Pops enjoyed the stuffed pork sandwich and fried oysters. Before we left, Pops and Shane got funnel cakes covered in powdered sugar, which both of them wore in a dusty coating on their shirts. We watched the National Oyster Shucking Championship, ate fantastic food, listened to bands, bought handmade baked good and crafts, and enjoyed the hospitality and company of good, down-to-earth people. It was a great time.

We were exhausted when we got home. We spent some time with Timber in the yard so he could run and play, but we turned in early that night. Shane and I slept in the large bedroom because it had the queen bed. I didn't tell Shane anything about the room, especially not the male spirit I had seen in the closet a few years earlier. I hoped that spirit had disappeared and we'd get a restful night's sleep, after the long drive down and back to Saint Mary's County.

Well, we had what I would consider the absolute worst night of sleep, even to this day. Within an hour of going to bed, we awoke to sounds of rattling on the windows. It sounded like someone was trying to push the metal screens in. Shane was a little freaked out, so he got up and peered out the window. The trees remained motionless, without the slightest sign of wind. We couldn't find the source, so we tried to go back to sleep.

I sat up in bed to read a book; I felt the hovering energy of the man in the closet. Shane said that the room felt weird and he couldn't sleep from the rattling of the windows. He rolled over and closed his eyes. A few moments later, the shade over the window closest to the bed rolled up on its own. Nanny loved roller shades and had them in all the bedrooms. Shane got out of bed and pulled the shade all the way down so it covered the windowsill. He got back in bed, pulled the covers to his neck, and nestled in his pillow. Less than five minutes later, the shade snapped all the way up to the top of the window, again. Shane frowned and rolled his eyes at me. He walked over to the shade and heaved it down once more. He got back into bed, yanked the covers up, and thrust his body on his side. As soon as he got comfortable, the shade rolled up again, revealing the dark night sky.

"These things suck," Shane said as he pulled the shade off the bracket. "Between this piece of crap," pointing to the plastic white shade in his hand, "and the screens rattling, we'll never get any sleep in this house." I didn't like the window without a shade or curtain; I felt like eyes were peering in at us, and based on the strange noises we heard that night, I knew spirits were probably there. Nanny had blue sheers on a curtain rod over the window, but they didn't offer much privacy. Shane grabbed a blanket off a chair in the room and he threw it over the curtain rod.

"This is total bullshit," Shane said as he got back into the bed. "We've been up here for almost two hours, and I haven't slept a bit." I wondered if I should tell him about the energy in the closet, but he was really annoyed and I thought it would make him angrier. I agreed it was annoying, and we both rolled over to get some sleep.

Around 3:00 am, we woke to the sound of knocking at the front door. Shane and I both got out of bed and stood at the top of the large oak staircase, which led directly to the front door. The house had a black wooden front door with a rectangular window in the upper portion. A screen door covered the main wooden door. As we sat on the top of the stairs, we had a clear view of the front porch through the door's window. The knocks were coming from the main front door, though the screen remained shut. It would be physically impossible for someone to knock on the front door without first opening the screen door. We sat at the top of the stairs, wondering what to do as the knocking continued.

Timber ran past us and darted down the stairs barking at the door with the fur raised on his back. We argued for a couple of minutes about who would venture down the stairs and retrieve the dog. Honestly, I was scared that if I got to the bottom of the stairs, the door might fly open and maybe even hit me in the face. Anything seemed possible based on the previous hours' course of events. We rock, paper, scissored for it, and I lost. I pleaded with Shane and he relented. Shane flew down the stairs as though running across hot coals. He scooped up our little puppy and bounded up the staircase once more. The knocking continued the entire time.

We wondered if this happened on a regular basis or if it had to do with us being in the house. We thought about waking Pops up, but he slept with a gun under his pillow. I know that sounds bizarre, but we feared being accidentally shot if we woke him from a sound sleep. He had limited vision due to advanced macular degeneration, which was part of the reason why he slept with a gun. I think the other part was because he felt scared without Nanny in the house. He never slept with a gun under his pillow when I visited from college. In the dark, Pops could only make out shadows. Shane and I weren't brave enough to wake him and test his aim.

We returned to our bedroom with Timber under Shane's arm. We agreed that eventually the knocking would stop, so we needed to try to get some sleep. Shane said that he suspected the house was haunted perhaps by Nanny. I chuckled nervously, because I didn't want to tell him what I knew—that the house was haunted because there was a spirit lingering in the closet. I felt like we were being visited by spirits that night, but they didn't feel familiar, certainly not my Nanny. Shane got very little sleep, and we had a five-hour drive home the following day, so I didn't think it was a good time to tell him about my sense of the spirit activity in and around that house.

Pops woke up early the next morning and cooked up his famous breakfast—scrambled eggs, sausage, and biscuits. At the table, Shane told Pops that we heard knocking on the front door early in the morning.

"What? There's no knocking around here. You must've been dreaming," he said. Shane glared over at me and I slowly focused on my coffee cup as I raised it to my lips. Even if the activity occurred on a regular basis, Pops was apparently oblivious to it because he slept through all the commotion.

On our drive home that morning, we decided not to stay in that house ever again. Actually Shane's words were that it was a "house of horrors" and we would never spend another night there. We agreed that we would drive down and pick Pops up so he could visit us, but we spent our last night in the house in Arlington. In retrospect, I don't think it was a "house of horrors," but I do think that perhaps me being a medium might have attracted other spirit energy in the area. It seemed like they were doing everything they could to get in and communicate.

I did suspect that the activity in our home with the alarm clocks etc, had something to do with Nanny, and I shared this with Shane. It started right after she died, so I thought she needed help. I began saying prayers for her. At the time, I felt overwhelmed with work and the new house. We had a bare yard that needed landscaping, sod, and most importantly, a fence. People were constantly walking through our yard to get to their houses. I recall one night we were eating dinner at the kitchen table and the woman from across the street was about three feet from our kitchen window. She stared in at us as she walked past our window, cutting through our yard to get to her house. I felt like a zoo animal behind a glass enclosure. We bought a fence the next weekend. That helped keep the people out of the yard, but we had very little furniture, flat white walls, and needed landscaping.

With all the chaos of settling into a new home, I didn't spend much time trying to reach out to Nanny. When I wasn't working, I was helping Shane paint the rooms or shopping to decorate. If I couldn't connect with Nanny right away, my mind jumped to other topics, like how I was going to afford everything to fill the rooms in the new house. I thought about her at night sometimes, right before I fell asleep.

One night, I had a vivid dream in which Nanny told me that my mother felt tremendous guilt about not being able to take care of her at the end of her life. My mother could not be there for Nanny because we lived in New Jersey. Also, my father had been ill and in the hospital for a few weeks, and my mother needed to take care of him until he recovered. But I guess in my mother's mind, she felt she had let Nanny down by not being there to take care of her. According to my Nanny, my mother had to choose between taking care of my father and taking care of her mother. If she chose one, then she had to sacrifice her time with the other. What my mother didn't foresee was that her time with Nanny would be cut short. In my dream, I saw my mother crying on her bed and she called out to Nanny. She asked Nanny to forgive her for not being there at the end of Nanny's life.

When I woke, I smelled Nanny's perfume—Christian Dior's Poison. It was very strong, as if someone had sprayed it over our bed. It made me recall the rounded purple bottle of it she kept on her cosmetic table. Shane woke and asked, "What's that sweet perfume smell? Did you spray something?" I smiled and told him Nanny had visited us. He shook his head and chuckled. Then he rolled over and fell asleep again. I thought it was interesting that Shane could smell the perfume, but I didn't mention it because he was sleeping and I didn't want to make a big deal about it.

I decided to call my mother that morning to tell her about my dream. It had been so vivid that it seemed less like a dream and more like a dream visit. I told her I dreamed about Nanny and what she shared about the guilt my mother felt. My mother started crying. I didn't ask any questions. I just let her experience the emotions, and I told her I had seen something specific. Her crying ceased, and I told her about seeing her on the bed and apologizing to Nanny for not being there. Then my mother sobbed uncontrollably. I waited quietly on the other end of the line for what seemed like a couple of minutes until she was able to get her emotions under control.

"Mom, did you talk to Nanny and ask her to forgive you for that?" I asked. She confirmed that she had asked Nanny to forgive her for not being able to take care of her.

"You should be happy, because she heard you and doesn't want you to feel bad about it," I told her. My mother said she was happy that Nanny had heard her apology, but she still missed her terribly. If I had been in the same room as my mother at that moment, I would have hugged her. I pictured her as a child reaching out for a hug—longing for the broken physical connection with her invisible mother. I told my mother that I loved her and asked her to be open to visits and communication from Nanny. She said she would try, although the shakiness in her voice didn't convince me.

My mother believed me, again. I had a true ally in my immediate family. I began to share my experiences with other family members. My older sister, who also shared the same abilities but suppressed them, supported and accepted the messages from Nanny. As a child, my sister too received visits from family and friends right before they died. She usually knew of a passing before anyone else. On one occasion, at the age of four, she informed my mother that their elderly neighbor wouldn't be attending a birthday party. When my mother asked why, my sister told her that the woman had died. A couple of hours later, a neighbor arrived with the news of the passing. When my mother asked my sister how she knew the neighbor died, she said, "she told me."

My younger brother still wanted nothing to do with mediumship. As soon as I started talking about it, he would put his hands over his ears. I learned to overlook the skepticism in some of my family members, because I realized it wasn't about me personally. Each person had his or her own level of awareness. The skeptics had the same dilemma regardless of whether or not I was in the picture. It was not about believing *me,* but rather believing in a tangible spirit world.

As extended family members passed, I had to deliver message to the living relatives. Over time, my living relatives realized I had a strange ability, and although they didn't understand it, they usually accepted the information from those who had passed.

In addition, I had my mother, sister, and of course, Shane to validate my credibility. The messages rarely meant anything to me personally; in fact, I often felt that the deceased spoke in code like Yoda from *Star Wars.* Sometimes I asked, "Are you sure you want me to say that? Why do I need to say this?" They never gave me the reason, and eventually I realized that it wasn't my job to censor or analyze the messages—I only needed to deliver them.

I thought that all families had a "family messenger." Looking back, I probably created this belief to help me accept my special abilities. However, it seemed plausible that there could be one messenger in each family. How else would they pass information from one realm to another? The visitors always said something validating that resonated with every recipient. Usually, it was something I did not know about—a specific nickname, an event that took place before I was born, or the location of a special gift or sentimental item. Because of the accuracy and specificity of the messages, my relatives grew to accept the information wholeheartedly. I still had a few doubters, but the list of believers began to outnumber the nonbelievers.

I enjoyed seeing grief-stricken people smile and happiness glimmering once again in their eyes. It felt safe to do this for family and maybe even friends, but I didn't want to see any strangers. I made sure that every night before bed I prayed, asking to be protected and for only loving, light-filled visitors. I never wanted to experience any negative energy or low vibrations. I pictured my house wrapped in a giant bubble of white light with the white energy seeping from the bubble, lighting every room in my house and through everyone in the house, including Timber. I asked for angels, guides, family members, friends, and all who dwelled in the light to guide and protect me always. My invocations were heard, and I was able to sleep peacefully without interruption from unwanted visitors. But I never knew what the morning would bring. What visitors would I see, hear, and feel? More importantly, what information would they want me to deliver?

FOUR

Teachers in Life and Death

I learned to manage my abilities through self-education and a little help from passed-on family members. I read lots of books on clairvoyance, mediumship, spirit guides, totem animals, prayer, chakras, alternative healing, energy balancing, and any other metaphysical topics I came across. These books gave me a broad understanding of universal spirituality, but as I read them, I often felt like I was remembering something I'd heard before, more than I was learning something new.

My deceased family members helped a great deal because I could ask them questions when they came through. They explained how some things worked on the other side.

I learned that often one's life path on earth plays a role in his or her path in the afterlife. In time, souls are assigned a path in which they can help other departed souls, people on earth, or work with spirit guides of the living.

A person's method of passing may have something to do with his or her role in the afterlife. For example, my cousin Gail, a magnificently loving mother, died of breast cancer at the young age of forty-one, leaving three beautiful children behind. On the other side, she transitions mothers who passed and left their children on the Earth plane.

On earth, Nanny had worked in a nursing home with dementia patients. On the other side, she works with spirit guides assigned to dementia-affected, geriatric adults on our plane. Spirit guides are souls that once lived on earth and are now in spirit form, assisting those in physical form.

Spirit guides are assigned to the living to help them on their life paths. In the case of dementia patients, they're often ready to pass on, but the body and mind connection isn't working properly, and sometimes they linger in a "failure to thrive" state rather than crossing over. Nanny works with the guides of these people, to help them cross over and move on. Life in spirit form continues on the other side.

Once we leave our body behind, the soul lives on and experiences, works, and evolves. The discarnate souls of our family and friends are always connected to us. Since they can transcend space and time, they're around us whenever we need them. Many people hang around right after they leave their bodies to help the family cope with the loss. In fact, they often enjoy attending their funeral events.

I learned this lesson from a dear friend, a teacher for me on earth and still an instructor from the beyond. John Budney was my boss for five of the eight years we worked together, and the first non-family member to come through after passing. Like a big brother, he always made me laugh— a real wise guy. He looked ordinary, with brown hair, a medium build, and about six feet tall, but his personality was extraordinary.

Everyone liked Budney—he was the class clown and life of the company. He told funny jokes, busted chops, acted goofy, and enlivened the workplace. But he had a serious side. We often discussed things he didn't share with the guys he managed. We talked about how much he loved his wife, Kitty, especially because she wouldn't put up with any crap from him, and how he drank on business trips to cope with the distance from his kids. Since he managed a sales force for the entire country, that meant he traveled often, and it pained him to call home and have his daughter always ask him when he would be back.

I could ask him for advice about professional things and he would give me honest guidance—no sugarcoating of course. I remember one time I had an issue with one of the regional vice presidents not allowing his sales reps to work my accounts. I asked John how I should handle the situation.

"Maybe if you'd stop being a bitch, more people will wanna work with you. Can't be a pit bull all the time. You gotta give these guys a little slack; they can't take constant pressure." I always took his advice because he had way more experience than me and he rarely stressed over interpersonal conflict. He was right—I felt that I had to put out the bitch-vibe or the men I worked with would treat me like a pretty moron. Truth be told, the job didn't fit my personality, and once John wasn't there to give me advice anymore, it became more evident.

During an annual management conference in January of 2004, the CEO announced John's promotion to senior vice president. Everyone congratulated him. Shortly after, he said he wanted to show me some new pictures of the kids in his office. We walked into John's office and he instructed me to close the door.

"So, what's up?" I asked. He leaned back on his chair with his arms crossed behind his head and smirked.

"I have cancer," he blurted out plainly.

"Very funny," I said. "Why would you joke about that, jackass?"

"I'm serious," he said, while smirking. He liked teasing, so I still thought he was pulling my leg. Then he dialed his wife, Kitty, and put her on speakerphone. I said hi and asked how the kids were doing. John told her that they'd announced his promotion. Then he told her that I didn't believe him when he said he had cancer. Kitty confirmed the diagnosis, as I sat back in my chair in silence and disbelief. I tried not to cry because I always wanted to seem like one of the guys. But I couldn't fight back the tears. I felt a single tear creep out of my left eye, sliding down my cheek. Then they slid down my face one by one. I quickly wiped them with the back of my hand, but they kept flowing, like water from a faucet. He chuckled.

"What are ya crying for?"

"I wasn't ready for that, you butt-face! I thought you were kidding!" He handed me a tissue and I dried my cheeks. John leaned forward, looked me straight in the eye, and told me with determination that he was going to fight it and beat it. I believed him; he was strong and could do it.

That year moved swiftly. John continued his job, though he had major surgery and many cancer treatments. We spoke often and joked around, but he didn't have his usual energy. The nature of our discussions were less work-related and more life-oriented. In one of our last conversations, he said that he wished he had worked less and spent more time with his kids. He said, "My main regret is that I won't be able to see them grow up." I listened in silence, trying to fathom the difficult realization he faced daily. I always said, "You can do this, John. You can beat it." He agreed. "Plus you can throw down the cancer card for anything. It's like a limitless credit card. 'Sorry I can't make quota this month...I got cancer,'" I said. I always threw in a wise-ass comment or joke at the end of every conversation just to make him laugh, but as he grew weaker I heard a distance in his voice.

In September of 2004, John was in and out of the hospital. We got word that he wasn't doing well. At that time, I said out loud, "John, if you need anything, let me know." I wasn't sure that he could hear me, but I just sent the message out to the universe anyway. I never had the opportunity to tell him that I was a medium, but I hoped he would somehow find out on his own as my family members had in the past.

One night, I dreamt vividly of John. At first I didn't recognize him with his frail build; he had lost all his hair, too. He told me that cancer was the worst thing he could have imagined. He wore a blue button-up shirt and black pants. I wasn't sure why, but something told me to take specific note of his outfit. He showed me pictures of some agents that worked for us. Agents were indirect sales representatives selling services for our company in exchange for large residual commissions. Since they weren't direct employees, John's team spent time taking the agents out to dinners and social events, ensuring they would bring their clients to our company rather than a competitor.

In most photos, the guys were hanging out, drinking scotch, and smoking cigars. One man was in all the pictures. I asked John who he was, and he told me the man's name. We will call him "Mike" for the story's sake. I never met Mike, but I knew of him, through John. He said that Mike was in danger of developing cancer. John asked me to get the message to Mike. John specifically said that if Mike didn't change his lifestyle, he would end up like

John. I agreed to deliver the message, although I wasn't sure how I'd get it to a complete stranger. I told John to let me know if he needed anything else.

I wrote down notes from the dream as soon as I woke. The next morning I checked my Blackberry to see if there was a company email regarding John's passing but there wasn't one. I wondered how I could've had such a vivid dream, which was more like a visit than a dream, when John was still alive. Usually, I only had those kind of experiences with people who had passed. It had never happened with someone who was still living. I waited all weekend, hearing nothing as I mulled over the dream details. They were so specific and I recalled all of them, but I dismissed it as a vivid dream. On Monday morning, I called a friend who worked at headquarters to see if he heard anything. He said Budney was still hanging on but as of Friday night (the night I had the dream), he had been basically in a morphine coma. I tried to make sense of the dream, and sent him positive thoughts. I hoped he received my message.

The following afternoon, one of the sales vice presidents flew in to see Budney. John waited for this person to say a final goodbye. Shortly after his visit, Kitty whispered in John's ear that it was "quittin' time" and just after 5:00 pm on September 21, 2004, he passed. The CEO sent out an email to the company announcing John's passing. I was alone in my house when I saw it. Tears flooded my eyes, as I read the message and acknowledged John's passing.

"John, if you need me, let me know," I said aloud for the second time. Just then, my son's toy camera sitting on the kitchen table went off by itself. When you pressed the button to take a picture, it made a shutter noise just like a real camera. The noise caught my attention, and I moved closer and inspected the toy. I picked it up and held it in my palm. "If that's you, John, set it off again to confirm." Again, the camera sounded. I smiled and said aloud, "If you need anything, you know where to find me." The little camera sounded a third time and a wave of comfort enveloped me. I knew John could reach me if he wanted to, and I believed he would be fine. However, I wasn't prepared for the funeral and the events that followed.

I struggled on the plane ride to Rochester. A host of emotions—sadness, confusion, and uncertainty—twisted my insides uncomfortably. I remembered happy times with John. I thought of the day I picked him up at the South Jersey office in my sporty new Lexus and we drove to a diner for breakfast. I opened the sunroof as we sped down a steep dip in the road. I gunned the gas, and we caught a little air. I glimpsed to the left and saw John's head pop up through the sunroof. When we landed he shouted at me.

"Tell me you honestly didn't see that dip!" I laughed and told him that was what he got for not wearing a seat belt with me. I'm pretty sure he always wore a seat belt after that incident. Remembering good times brought a smile to my face. Then my thoughts shifted from past to future. I wondered how everything would change. For me, a sudden difference was the absence of John picking me up at the airport. Anytime I flew in, John met me at the airport and then we either went to breakfast or lunch, depending on the time. A couple of times, we went to lunch at the Leiderkranz Club, also known as "the club"—a local restaurant he frequented with his family. The nondescript club had dark walls, a bar, and about ten tables with vinyl-covered chairs. Its basic, home-cooked fare matched the family-style ambiance.

No lunch at the club for me this time. I rented a car with a little trepidation, took out my printed directions, and drove straight to the funeral home. I honestly felt a little nervous because I didn't know my way around the area and I couldn't call John's cell phone to ask him for directions. I arrived at the funeral home in one piece. As I parked, I noticed a line of visitors forming outside the building. Like I said earlier, everyone loved John. I met one of the women who worked in the corporate office, and we waited together in the line. John's family had made a video of him with lots of pictures set to the music of Frank Sinatra's "My Way." The video played continuously on television screens in the funeral home hallway.

John's family, friends, colleagues, customers, and sales agents from all over the country lined the walls. Kitty and John's parents greeted people in a sort of receiving line. As I stepped through the room's doorway, I caught a glimpse of the casket and noted that they had dressed John in the dark blue shirt and black pants I had seen him wearing in the dream. At that moment, I realized it was a visit, not just a vivid dream. Suddenly, his passing hit me like a ton of bricks. Tears streamed down my face, and I began sobbing. I realized that my surrogate big brother would no longer be on Earth. The whole experience seemed surreal.

When we reached the receiving line, I dried my eyes and introduced myself to John's parents. I had met Kitty a few times at social events, but figured she was overwhelmed that day and might not have recognized me. I introduced myself again, and she hugged me, saying, "Oh Anysia, John loved you." Of course, when she said that, I started crying, again. I did manage to say that I couldn't believe how he had suffered, and Kitty replied that he put up a good fight. Stopping at the casket seemed too overwhelming, so I sat in a chair next to a friend and colleague. She gave me a hug and passed me a box of tissues. I was glad to have her there; she was sweet and helped me pull myself together.

The next day, I said goodbye to John at the funeral mass. His best friend delivered one of the most honest eulogies I had ever heard. As I listened to him honor John in words, I realized that John had a special gift; he mastered the art of friendship. All of those people attended the funeral to remember a good friend. He didn't care about race, religion, gender, economic background—if he liked someone, he was a friend to them till the end.

John always told me that he believed in God and that he even had an aunt who was a nun. Of course, I didn't believe him. At the funeral, I saw his aunt standing there in her black and white habit. I wondered what other things he had spoken in truth that I misinterpreted as jokes. I cried as I drove back to the airport with a couple of vice presidents from our California office in my car. I had given up on the futile attempt of hiding tears. It had nothing to do with being a woman, but everything to do with being human. One of the VPs sitting in the front seat cried his eyes out, too. I offered him a box of tissues. I really couldn't believe that I would never see John again. But I hoped that in time, I would hear from him again.

FIVE

A Servant in the Spirit World

One month after John passed, I heard Frank Sinatra's "My Way" playing on my car radio as I drove to work. I knew John was with me because it was a mainstream radio channel, not a mellow music one.

"Okay, you got my attention, what do you need?" I heard John's voice as he instructed me to buy a dozen white roses for Kitty. He asked me to send them from him. Of course I told him that I wouldn't send them from him, but I would order them. I asked him why he needed the flowers. He wanted Kitty to know that he was with her, helping her through her grief.

"Don't cheap out on me, kid!" he urged. I assured him my hesitations weren't about money but were more about Kitty perceiving me as a crazy person. John said, "You'll see. In time, you and Kitty will be friends."

"She doesn't even know me," I said.

"She will know you, through me," he said. I had the sudden realization that John pegged me as his personal earthly servant. I should have added a caveat during his last visit. I said, "If you need anything let me know." But I should have said, "If you need anything *reasonable*…let me know." I dropped $85 and sent the flowers from my family. I didn't care what he said. I wasn't sending a widow a dozen white roses with her deceased husband's name on the card. She could perceive it as some type of sick joke. Eventually I would try to find a way to let her know the flowers were from John. I knew she liked them because we received a thank-you note shortly after I sent them to her. A couple of weeks later, I woke to hearing "My Way" again. It blared in my ears like someone had a speaker on my pillow. I put my hands over my ears and sat up in bed.

"What the hell?" I shouted.

"Stop ignoring me!" I heard John say.

"I'm not ignoring you. It's called sleeping, something you have to do when you're in a body. Obviously you forgot about that part," I said. My husband woke and asked who I was talking to. I told him John had been here for a visit. Shane didn't seem surprised; he knew about all the other John incidents over the past months. He rolled over and went back to sleep. I thanked God for sending me such and easygoing husband. Not many men would be able to handle such ghostly visits with patience and ease. Either he really loved me or he had a tremendous ability to block things out. I had hoped it was the former over the latter.

On my way to work that morning, I heard that Sinatra song again, on the radio. Then I heard John say to call Ricky, one of his closest buddies at work, and tell him that he was okay. I loved Ricky; he was an honest, caring, family man. But I wasn't sure he could handle what I was about to tell him.

"I'm not doing it," I said. "There's no way he'll believe me."

"He'll believe you because it's me," John assured. I shut off the car radio.

"Listen, I don't mind helping you out, but if I wind up looking like a nut job, I'm done helping. You better have my back!" I said. John chuckled and assured me that he wouldn't leave me hanging out to dry, although the chuckle made me question his sincerity.

When I got to my office in North Jersey, I called Ricky and told him that I needed to go over something with him. After a few moments of small talk about families and work, I briefly explained that I was a medium and that I had spoken with John since his passing. Anxiety bubbled in my chest and I took a few small breaths like I might run out of air. Ricky was Jewish and I didn't know his religion's take on the afterlife. He listened quietly and surprisingly, he believed everything I said. I told him the whole story from the dream to Kitty's white rose delivery. He thought we should tell Kitty. I told him that I wasn't ready to talk to her about it because I didn't know her well enough. Plus, I didn't want to interfere with her grieving process. I thought I would wait a bit, until her wounds of his passing had time to heal. Ricky didn't put up much of an argument about it.

He wanted to deliver the message to the agent, Mike. I thought it was a great idea since I had no way of contacting the man, and I had promised I would somehow get the message to him. Ricky actually called Mike in Florida and told him what John said. Ironically, unbeknownst to both of us, Mike had a scare with cancer, when John was diagnosed in January of 2004. He didn't share the cancer scare with many people, but John knew. The message from John hit home, and he thanked Ricky for making the call. I never asked Ricky what he said to Mike, but his faith in John amazed me. He never questioned John's information for a second; John was right about him. I felt relieved, though I personally didn't deliver the message.

Through Ricky, the information was delivered and well received. I thanked Ricky for helping me and believing. He modestly downplayed the whole thing. Like I said, Ricky was honest and caring, and I was truly grateful for his assistance.

Ricky told me he had a picture of John on his desk that he looked at every morning. He said it made him feel like John was always with him.

"The next time you talk to John, tell him I want a sign. I want a sign with a picture." I promised Ricky I would give John the message, although I was quite sure John had heard the whole conversation.

A week later, while in my office reading a report, my email launched and a folder called "John" (where I saved all his funny emails) opened without me touching the keyboard.

"You got my attention, what's up?" John told me to call Ricky and ask if he got his sign. I dialed Ricky's office and got his voicemail. Then I emailed him and asked the question, "Did you get your sign?" He sent me an email back asking, "What sign?" I sent another one off saying, "Did you get your sign with a picture from John?" Ricky sent an email back asking me to call him and he forwarded me his cell phone number. I wondered why I had to call and why he just couldn't send a reply, letting me know if he got a sign or not. I called the number, and he answered on the first ring.

"Did you get your sign with a picture?" I asked. Ricky said that he had to sit down and he asked if I knew where he was. I told him that I had no idea where he was, but I really just wanted him to answer my question. I felt like I was pulling teeth. How many times did I have to ask?

Ricky went on to say that he had just left an agent's office, and the woman there gave him a plaque about friendship with a picture of John on it. He had just walked out of the building as he read my first email. He was sitting down on a curb in New York City taking it all in.

"Well, I guess you got your sign." I said. He told me to thank John for him. "Thank him yourself, I'm sure he's listening," I said. I could tell Ricky felt overwhelmed; he seemed to be catching his breath and his voice sounded shaky.

"Thanks John, for my sign and for being a great friend," he said out loud. A chill ran through me as Ricky spoke because this situation demonstrated how mediumship could really help people here on earth. Ricky still wanted me to contact Kitty, but I said I needed a little more time to figure out how to approach her.

A week went by, and then while sitting in my den one day, the little toy camera went off several times. I walked over to it and picked it up. The camera was still going off when I heard John say to send the camera to Kitty.

"First you want me to send your wife a dozen roses and sign the card from you and now you want me to send her a toy camera? Are you trying to land me in the mental ward? This is crazy. No more favors for you!"

"Hey, you said if I need *anything*. I need you to do this." John said. He explained that it would help him communicate with Kitty. I said I'd think about it. Quite honestly, I thought if it would get him off my back so he could communicate with her directly instead of using me as his personal messenger, I'd overnight the damn thing. John had become an invisible stalker. On my drive to work, I mulled over scenarios of getting the camera to Kitty. I tried to decipher which one would give the least impression of insanity, but couldn't decide.

I called Ricky and asked for advice, since he was the only person at work that knew about it. He said that no matter what, I had to send the camera. I agreed with him. He offered to call Kitty and explain the events to her. I agreed because he knew her better than I did, and I lacked the courage to do it myself. I thought he would have waited a few days but he called me back about thirty minutes later and told me to call Kitty.

"She wants to talk to you, now," Ricky said. I wondered if she might yell at me or maybe even think I was a little crazy. My nerves jostled around in my stomach like I was on a turbulent airplane.

"You're sure she wants to talk to me?" I asked in disbelief.

"Yeah, she said for you to call her. She's home now." I told Ricky that I was scared of Kitty's possible reaction. He told me not to be worried; she was excited to speak with me. I promised to call him right after my conversation with her.

Dialing Kitty's number, my hands trembled. As I heard her voice on the other end, a sudden serenity enveloped me. I felt John's presence and I knew he would help me. The conversation began with friendly talk about our kids and then Kitty asked me about hearing from John. I conveyed the dream story before John passed and the toy camera incident. I also mentioned the outfit he wore in the dream, which was the same one he wore at his funeral. I asked her why she selected that blue shirt for him.

"I don't know. I had a different shirt in my hand and something made me go back to the closet and pick out that blue shirt," she said. I think John had something to do with her going back and picking up that blue shirt. I briefly reiterated Ricky's story because I was sure he relayed it to her or else she would not have wanted to speak with me. As I cruised through the details, John began saying things that he wanted me to convey. At this point, I relented because I knew he was there to help me console her and validate his visit.

I told Kitty that John was with us and had some things to share. He showed me an image of his daughter in a very specific Christmas dress. It had a black velvet, long-sleeved top with a taffeta bottom that had a gold overlay. As I described the princesslike dress, Kitty said that it was the exact dress she purchased for her daughter. I asked if John saw it before he passed and she said she bought it in November after he died. She said tearfully that she was having a hard time not putting his name on that year's Christmas card. Every year, they sent out a picture card of the kids with all of their names on it. John suggested that she could leave his name on it or put "The Budney Family." Kitty admitted that she had not thought of putting the family name, and she would consider it.

John showed me a picture of his family sitting in a pew in church and he was seated on the end. I told her I was not sure why he was showing it. Kitty knew right away. They had gone to church weekly as a family, and since his passing, she had a hard time taking the kids back to church. She knew it was his way of telling her that he wanted them to go to church. John also said that he wanted me to send Kitty the camera and a song for his daughter—John Mayer's "Daughters." I told Kitty that I needed to send the items to her, and that he promised to set off the camera. We agreed to speak again, once he set the camera off for her. In hindsight, I should have asked him when exactly he would set it off for her.

In November of 2005, a year after John's passing, I flew to Orlando for an annual conference. Many of John's former direct reports were there. Jay was a manager under John and a really good guy. He approached me at the conference and asked me to reach out to his brother who has passed on. He heard through Ricky that John had visited me, and he really wanted to hear from his brother. I told him that I wasn't sure that it would work because John was the first non-family member who had ever come through. I told him that I didn't think I could do it.

"No problem, I just thought I'd ask," Jay replied, but I could read the lines of disappointment written in his expression. I really was being honest—I didn't think I could communicate with total strangers. I had seen them in the past but had never spoken with them. I lacked confidence in my abilities.

That night, I went back to my hotel room to work on my creative thesis for my master's degree. I was studying for my MFA in creative writing full-time while working full-time as well. As I wrote into the hours of the early morning, I thought about Jay's request.

"Just help him out," I heard John command. I sat with the request for a moment, thinking I would just try it. If Jay's brother didn't come through, at least I could say I tried. I wasn't sure how to reach out to him, but I had read that some mediums called out telepathically to people using the deceased person's full birth name and either their birth or death date. Some mediums believe you need to be very specific when reaching out. If you only say "John Smith," you could get every John Smith who has passed on. Using the birth name and birth/death dates ensured contacting the correct soul.

I ran into Jay the next morning at breakfast. I mentioned that I would try to reach his brother and conveyed what information I needed. That night, at a company dinner, Jay passed me a folded cocktail napkin with the information. I could see a glimmer of hopeful light in his eyes as we parted ways. When I went back to my room, I reached out to his brother and wrote down several pages of notes. He came up right away, and I received some visual images of him. He was funny and charismatic, the type of person who could get along with anyone. I saw him walking through a hotel lobby. To the left behind the front desk was a glass sculpture kind of like a sun. I recognized it because I had been at that hotel a month earlier for work. It was Foxwoods Resort Casino in Connecticut. I saw him leave the lobby wearing a t-shirt and jeans, but he didn't have a bag. He gave me some more information for Jay, and I thanked him for visiting and sharing the information with me.

At that point, I realized that I didn't have to worry about my own confidence because the process had nothing to do with me. I was just the conduit through which information flowed from one part of the universe to another. The next day, I gave the notes to Jay, who was thrilled—his brother shared information that only the two of them knew. I told him I saw his brother walking through Foxwoods Resort Casino, and I wondered what he was doing there. Jay replied that his little brother was a bartender there. That tidbit of information was validation for both of us.

Four months after Jay asked me to speak with his brother, I got a message from John Budney for Jay. There were some things going on at work, and John wanted Jay to know everything would be okay. John said, "tell him to have a scotch on the rocks for me." I had never seen Jay drink scotch; he usually drank beer. I called him and gave him the message.

"Why is he saying the scotch thing? I thought you were a beer guy?" I asked. Jay knew exactly what that meant. He had given John a bagpipe shotglass that played bagpipe music. Sometimes John would call Jay on the phone and not say a word, but just have the shooter playing its music. It became a joke between them. When John passed, Kitty gave it back to Jay and he put it on a scotch bottle in his house.

The comment was John's way of letting Jay know he had the bagpipe shooter.

Jay contacted Kitty to tell her the story, and she emailed me saying that John had finally set the camera off for her. I couldn't believe he waited a whole year to set it off. I thought he would have set it off the say after she received it in the mail. In the email, Kitty said that she went into the living room and asked a question about whether or not she should do something and the camera went off. She was thrilled that he finally set it off, and she instructed the kids not to be scared if they heard it go off. She told them it meant Daddy was around them. I felt relief that he finally set it off, but slightly annoyed that he took his time doing it. But John would not be told when or how to do anything, which is why "My Way" was an appropriate song for him.

In June of 2006, Jay forwarded me an email sent from Budney's work email address to Jay's work email. The subject was 57657. The body of the email was blank. He asked me what it was about. I asked how he got an email from John's work address, because it had been disabled for over two years. I wanted to say, "Why the heck are you asking me why you got that email?" Five minutes after he sent it to me, I had a message in my inbox from me to me with the same number in the subject line: 57657. I realized something strange was happening. It was weird for several reasons. First, I didn't send that message to myself. Second, John Budney's email address was disabled after he died. Third, we had no idea what that number meant, and lastly, we checked other people in the company, but we were the only two to get the email.

A couple of minutes later, I checked my program email. I had two company email addresses—one for my name and the other for the program I managed—and there was another one in the program inbox sent to and from the program email address and the subject was 57657. When I opened the email, the only thing in the body was a number 455. I knew what this number meant—4/5/05 was the day the company cancelled my program and I signed my offer letter to move into marketing. It was not a good day for me and when I saw that number in the program inbox, it struck a chord. I forwarded both of my emails to Jay and I asked John what it was all about. He said things weren't going well for Jay and he wanted to let him know that he was around to help. I asked him how he could do that with our emails.

"We can do all kinds of crazy shit," he said chuckling. I didn't refute this because I knew they could set things off and basically do anything to get the living to wake up and know they were being visited. I called Jay and gave him John's message. He was thrilled to know John was helping him. As soon as I hung up with Jay, a new message appeared in my inbox. It was addressed to me, sent from me, and the subject line was 57657. The body had only one number 969. The 969 had no specific significance to me, but I knew this was John's way of thanking me for giving Jay the message.

That Christmas, I received a card from Kitty and the kids. We exchanged cards every year and wrote a family up-date on the back. On the back of her card, she thanked me for sending the camera—it was the greatest gift. She said John used it to communicate with them often. She invited me to call her to discuss the details.

I called her the next day, and she shared all the details of how John had managed to use the camera as a vehicle for communicating with her and the kids. She said all their family and friends knew about the camera. After I got off the phone, I thanked John for using the camera and for helping me, because everything he said would happen did. Most of all, he always had my back through everything.

SIX

Smudging
the Garage

After John's visits, a lot of mysterious things happened, though it took a while for me to fit the puzzle pieces together. It began with the laundry room door. One night as Shane and I settled on the couch to watch a movie, the metal door connecting the laundry room and garage creaked loudly. Shane made his way to the laundry room and found it slightly ajar. Timber followed behind Shane— hair raised on his back, flashing his teeth, and growling ferociously. No one was there, though Timber continued snarling. Shane seemed perplexed, scratching his head. He pushed the door closed, gave it an extra shove with his palm, and locked it. He said that he might not have closed it all the way when he let Timber in the house earlier.

"Maybe the wind pushed it open," he said. It struck me as a little odd, but I dismissed it because I wanted to continue relaxing and watching the movie with my husband—a rare moment for a mom and dad with a new baby. He snuggled next to me and we enjoyed our popcorn and movie.

The next morning, I staggered into the kitchen in my sleepy stupor, longing for my cup of coffee. Shane always set the timer the night before, so the coffee would be ready as soon as we entered the kitchen. The smell of French roast with hints of cinnamon and nutmeg greeted my nasal passages, signaling a wake-up call to my brain.

I gazed at the translucent steam clouds billowing from the hot cup, warming my fingertips. As I glanced out the window, the sun unfolded like petals on a bright yellow sunflower that melted the frost-tipped blades of grass.

A loud squeak interrupted my tranquility and as I turned my head, I noticed the laundry room door was open again, though it wasn't windy. Timber ran over and growled at the door. I patted his head and told him he was a good boy. He wagged his tail and plopped down on his pillow.

As I inspected the door handle, a faint smell of roses floated in the room, and I wondered if it was one of the laundry detergents on the shelf. I opened the green bottle and sniffed, but it smelled of apples. The white bottle was scent-free; I used it for the baby's laundry.

I saw Shane lock the door the night before, but perhaps he'd unlocked it when he left for work. I closed the door and went upstairs to shower. I turned the shower on and brushed my teeth as the water heated up. When I stepped into the shower, frigid water pelted my skin as if I had just walked naked in a hailstorm. I shut the shower off and wrapped my goose-bumped body in my bathrobe.

I ran down to the garage and checked the hot water heater. The pilot light remained lit but the temperature dial was turned all the way down. I hadn't touched the dial, and I had taken a hot shower the night before. Once again, the faint smell of rose petals wafted past my nose. I turned the dial up on the water heater and heard it kick on. I recalled that last week, I had come downstairs in the morning and the kitchen light wouldn't turn on. I had to go into the garage and flip the circuit breaker. Between the time I came downstairs that day for my coffee and the time I left for work, I had to switch the breaker back five times because the kitchen lights kept going out. I remembered smelling roses in the garage that day, but I was so rushed for work, I did not have time to consider the source.

When I came home that same night, I had to switch the circuit breaker for the downstairs bathroom as well because the light wouldn't come on. Our house was only a few years old. We were the first owners and had never had any electrical issues. My stomach twisted in knots; I realized that between the patterns of activity in the garage last week and the activity this week, someone or something was trying to get my attention.

I had read about the Native American technique of smudging to clear the energy in a space. I had never tried, but I thought it might be a good idea to clear the garage to get rid of any stagnant or negative energy. I dressed my son, Brayden, and got him ready to visit my parents' house. They watched him three days a week, when I went to the office.

On my way home from work that night, I stopped at a small New Age store that sold books, crystals, and other things I couldn't find in any other store. They had a few varieties of smudge sticks, so I asked the man behind the counter for assistance. He gave me a rudimentary lesson in smudging, and sent me on my way with my sage.

By the time I got done cleaning up from dinner and putting Brayden down for bed that night, I didn't have the energy to smudge the garage. I told Shane about the method I learned and my suspicions of our unexpected guest that had take up residency in the garage. He didn't argue the possibility. He had witnessed many strange occurrences in our marriage and learned not to dismiss anything as coincidence. Something was different about this situation—the activities over the course of the past two weeks had been ongoing, and the energy seemed persistent. I felt a little uneasy because I didn't know what kind of energy was lingering out there.

Before I left for work the next morning, I led Timber through the garage to the backyard and decided to speak aloud to my unwanted visitor.

"Listen up! I know you're here and you're not welcome. I'm smudgin' this place with a ton of sage tonight and you're goin', whether you like it or not," I said with my arms crossed as I leaned against the garage wall. Of course, I didn't hear any retort, so I figured my attempt at scaring the entity worked. But Timber cowered with the hair up on his back as I walked toward him. He squinted his eyes as if straining to see something and backed away from me. I leaned down to pet him and he ran away whimpering through the yard. I looked around at my surroundings and there was just the open side garage door. I realized Timber got a glimpse of whatever had taken up residency in our garage. I panicked, my heart beat rapidly in my chest. Apparently my little announcement had no effect even though I assumed an assertive pose.

I called Timber in the house and locked the door. I grabbed the infant carrier, flung the diaper bag over my shoulder, and headed for my car. As I put the key in the ignition, the garage door opened by itself. The two-car garage had an automatic door opener on the left side and a manual door on the right side. The manual side was open about four feet. I had just been in the garage, and the door was closed and locked. I had no idea how it opened or how I didn't hear it open.

Suddenly, the manual door slammed down to the ground. Within a minute, the manual door opened again on its own. I bit my lower lip to stop it from quivering as I felt fear climb up my spine and paralyze me. I sat in the car and cried for a minute, wondering what to do. I thought I was in over my head.

I decided to drive to my parents' house, a couple of miles away. I had to drop Brayden off and thought I could bring my dad back to help me get the door shut and smudge the garage, though I wouldn't tell him the part about the sage. I needed to lie to him to get him over to my house; I couldn't tell him there was a spirit in my garage. My father was a conservative Catholic and the whole spirit thing didn't fit into his world. Fortunately, Brayden was sleeping soundly in his infant carrier, so he wasn't aware of what was happening or the level of fear that pervaded every cell in my body. On the drive over, I rehearsed the possible conversation with my father in my head.

When I arrived at my parents' house, I found my father sitting in his chair reading the morning paper. As I placed Brayden's car seat on the couch, he raised his eyes from the paper and knitted his brows a bit. He glanced at his wrist checking the time.

"This is late for you. Don't you need to be at work by now?" he asked.

"Actually, I need you to go back to the house with me because I have a little problem with the garage door," I replied.

"Sure. Do I need to bring any tools?" he asked, folding his paper.

"No, you just need to help me pull it shut," I said. Just then, my mother entered the kitchen carrying a basket full of dirty laundry.

"Morning, Mom." She smiled and set the basket gently on the floor and then tiptoed over to the couch where Brayden was sleeping. She smiled admiringly at him like a proud grandmother would over her first grandchild.

"I'll have to go over Anysia's to help her with the garage door. I'll be right back," my father said. She nodded and carefully tucked in an extra receiving blanket around Brayden's little body like a piecrust fitted around a sweet fruit pie.

On the brief drive to my house, my father suggested the door might be jammed.

"Nothing a little WD-40 won't fix," he added. When we pulled into the driveway the manual door was still open. After I parked the car, I hit the garage door opener and opened the left door, so we could gain full access to the garage.

"Maybe that manual door is jammed," my father said.

"Maybe, but we never open it, so I'm not sure how it could jam on its own or jam open. I also have another little problem. You're not going to believe this, but I have some type of spirit activity here involving that door and I didn't want to come back by myself," I said, fighting back tears, though I couldn't control my quivering lower lip. He gazed at me with a quizzical look with his eyes deep set and a frown of disbelief.

"Are you telling me that a spirit opened that manual door?" he asked with a wrinkled face emphasizing the creases in his forehead. I nodded and wiped a few of my tears with my fingertips.

"I need your help shutting the door, and I may need to burn some sage in here. I didn't want to be alone because this spirit is persistent and I need your help with the door," I said desperately.

"Well do whatever you need to do and I'll be right here in the car if you need anything," he said fastening his seat belt.

"I need you in the garage with me because I'm scared. This entity isn't a relative. Please come with me," I begged. My father looked at my eyes, and a gentle smile grew across his face.

"Okay, they don't want anything with me anyway. I'll just be the tall stupid guy who can't see ghosts," he said in a chuckle. We got out of the car and my father walked over to the manual door. He pulled it down and locked it from the inside. I instructed my father to stay in the garage while I ran into the house to grab a white candle, sage, and a box of matches. On my way out of the house, I heard a door slam.

"What was that noise?" I asked as I entered the garage.

"The side garage door just opened and slammed shut on its own. I saw it with my own eyes," he said sporting the deer-in-headlights expression as he pulled his rosary beads out of his pocket. "Why does it smell like you've been storing roses out here?" he asked. I was surprised he could smell the rose scent.

"Maybe you're more spiritual than you think. The rose smell is connected to the spirit. I began smelling it as all these things started happening in the garage," I said. He frowned and rolled his eyes. I struck a match and lit the white candle. Then I dipped the sprig of sage into the flame and the edges lit up in a deep orange. I blew out the flame and a thin line of smoke wafted through the air. I walked through the garage blowing the sage smoke into all corners while instructing all negative and stagnant energy to leave. I looked up at my father, who nervously rolled his rosary beads between his middle finger and thumb. I actually wondered if it would create enough friction to emit a spark.

"Where did you learn that little incantation you're saying? You sound like a witch," he said.

"It's just a type of prayer, Dad. The sage gets rid of negative and stagnant energy."

"That's not Catholic," he said. I reminded him that the Catholic religion didn't recognize spirit communication or existence of spirit presences on the Earth plane.

"We obviously know they're missing the mark on that based on what we're dealing with right now," I said.

"We'll...just finish it up. This stuff stinks and I need to get back to my paper," he said. I knew this experience was a bit much for my father, and I appreciated him helping. But the situation gave him tangible evidence of the spirit world, which was something he had never experienced before. After I finished smudging the garage, I blew out the candle and closed the manual door and locked it. We got back into the car and I hit the garage door opener but nothing happened—the door wouldn't close.

"Guess that sage doesn't work," my father said in a high-pitched voice. "What happens now?"

"I don't know but I can tell you that this spirit's annoying me. I'm not being bossed by a spirit in my own home," I said. We walked back into the garage because I needed to get the door shut. At that point, my six-foot-four father put his rosary beads around his neck and stood like a stone statue at the garage entrance. I tried to work the garage door opener from inside the garage but it wouldn't budge.

"You need to go! I don't want you here," I called out to the entity. As I turned around, I thought I saw my father edging his way back to the car. He seemed closer to the car than he had been a couple of minutes earlier. I felt like he was playing the child's game of "Red Light Green Light" back to the car. Each time I glanced behind me, he was closer to the car than he had previously been. I felt a little bad for exposing him to this situation, but I couldn't foresee that we would run into such complications. I thought we would come back to the house and shut the door. I expected that we'd be on our way to his house within ten minutes. I had no idea I'd be smudging with him there.

I finally got the garage door closed from the inside. I was going to tell my dad that we should go out through the side garage door, but when I looked up, I realized he was already in the car. As I stood in the yard and pulled the side garage door closed, I felt someone pulling against it. The rose smell enveloped me. Then I heard a woman's voice pleading with me. The voice—loud and clear—sounded as though the woman was physically standing right next to me. She said that I was her only hope. I continued my struggle to pull the door shut as the woman spoke. She said she had committed suicide and then a heavy wave of sad energy flooded me. I won the tug-of-war and closed the door, but my mind tangled in knots as this new experience puzzled me. I clearly heard this woman, though I had no apparent relation to her.

In the car, I thanked my father for helping me and staying by my side (for most of the experience). He smiled and his stark silence led me to believe he would try to erase the situation from his memory. I dropped him off at his house and headed to work.

On the drive to work, the woman told me her name telepathically. She said that her name was Kathleen. I got a visual image in my third eye of a medium-built woman with short, mousy brown hair. She said she passed at the age of forty. Her recent death explained why the sage didn't do much. She wasn't negative energy or stagnant (energy that lingered in a place for a number of years).

"Why can't you just move on and follow the light?" I asked with my mind. The woman asked what light I was talking about. "You know...the light! When people die they see a bright light and a long tunnel. If you follow it, you'll see your passed-on family members. Is any of this ringing a bell or sounding familiar?"

"All I see is darkness, and I'm completely alone. The only light I've seen is the one around your house," the woman said. I had no idea what light she was talking about. Perhaps she was referring to the porch light in the front of the house. If that little light attracted her, I wondered what other types of energy it could draw to my home. Perhaps it allured spirits with the same magnetism that it had with moths and other flying insects in the dark of night.

I knew from passed-on family members that every person crossing over from physical to spirit form had other spirits waiting for them. The other spirits could include guides, loved ones, and friends in spirit form. I wondered if she was in complete darkness, cut off from her passed-on loved ones as a result of her taking her own life. I also questioned why she was still hanging around of the Earth plane after she passed. This was all quite new to me; as it was the first contact I had with someone who had committed suicide. She was also the first non-family member or close friend spirit I encountered.

"I didn't really mean to kill myself. I want to move on, but I don't know how to do it," she said. "Please help me."

"I'd like to help you, but I can't. You see I can only communicate with relatives because I'm the universal family communicator. I've been doing it since I was a toddler. Every family has one—quite normal. You need to find the one in your family and they'll help you," I said.

"If you can only communicate with family members, then how can you communicate with me?"

"Not sure. This is a first for me, and I really don't know what's going on. I'm wondering if it's some kind of mistake. Maybe you should look for a professional medium to help you," I said.

I spent the rest of the day focusing on my work, which included lengthy conference calls that sucked up most of my energy. Between my morning calls, I ate my lunch at my office desk, my mind tumbling through possible scenarios of how this spirit might have found me. Perhaps she lived in my town or was related to someone living in the same town. Maybe she knew my family. There had to be a connection. A complete stranger wouldn't just find me, regardless of the light around the house she had referenced.

During my drive home, I thought about Kathleen and whether or not I should help her. If I didn't help cross her, she would probably linger in the garage. But I had never crossed anyone over, so I wasn't sure how to do it. I thought if I meditated and asked a passed-on relative to assist in the process, we could get her across. Just then, I felt something thin and cold—a plastic cord like the kind connecting a phone or cable to a wall—around my neck and I couldn't swallow. I didn't know what was happening. All of the sudden, the cord tightened, and I couldn't breathe for about five seconds. I gripped at my neck, which caused me to swerve into the next traffic lane—but nothing was around my neck. I quickly pulled my car to the shoulder and stopped driving. I started hyperventilating, though the cord feeling dissipated. I realized this woman was telling me that she hung herself.

As I sat in my car on the side of the parkway, my mind flashed fearful images from when I was a little girl and random strangers had materialized in my room. They appeared when I slept. I would see them as I waited for sleep or when I woke. I always told them to go away because they scared me. I didn't want to be that scared little girl anymore. I needed to release those old memories and patterns. I needed to help Kathleen. However, I also had to set some ground rules in the process. I composed myself and pulled back on to the road.

"Let's get a few things straight. I won't allow you or any other spirit to impose your method of passing on me. You shouldn't do it to anyone. Not only is it completely rude but you could've caused a serious car accident. I understand your need to communicate information, but it could've been sent with a visual image, or you could have communicated that information telepathically." Kathleen apologized and said that she didn't mean to cause any harm. I believed her; we were both "newbies" at this, learning from our mistakes. "I'm going to help you get across tonight, when I get home."

As soon as I got home, I fed Timber in the yard. Shane was picking Brayden up from my parents' house. I walked into the kitchen and poured myself a glass of water. The door between the laundry room and garage opened by itself, and Timber ran over to it growling.

"You don't have to open the door. As a spirit, you can go just go through the wall if you want," I said.

"I didn't want to just walk into your house, plus I was a little scared of dogs in my life," she said.

"Well I don't mind if you just pop in. Timber can't hurt you, though he does see you," I said. I told her we would go upstairs to my home office and cross her. I worked from home two days a week, so I had a dedicated room with my computer and work equipment. As I ascended the stairs to my office, I lit a small white candle. I perceived the presence of my Nanny by my side, pulsating in a bright magenta color. My body bubbled with a strong, loving current. I thanked her for being with me when I needed her, and I told her I loved her. I dipped a smudge stick in the candle flame and blew the smoke into the corners of the room while saying a prayer to God for protection and light. I sat down in Nanny's armchair and a burst of heat brushed across my face, followed by a strong scent of roses that filled the space, signaling Kathleen's presence. A soft, undulating energy vibrated around me, and I knew I was protected.

I asked Nanny to send me a sign when she was ready to begin the process. A warm breeze grazed my hands, although the windows were shut. It was followed by a cold blast, which gave me chills. I knew this was Nanny's sign.

I'm not sure how I knew to do the next part. Perhaps it was my guides (though I didn't know much about them at the time) who gave me the information about envisioning the tornado of light. I pictured a tornado of brilliant white light spinning in a clockwise direction around the entire house. I breathed quickly, as my breath seemed directly connected to the tunnel's speed. As my respiration rate increased, the whirlwind gained speed. It spun faster and brighter, and I could barely breathe until I saw a translucent spirit fly out the top and funnel up to the heavens. Then the tunnel slowed, as did my breathing. It disappeared, and I relaxed for a few minutes. The energy in the room felt light and peaceful.

As I sat in Nanny's favorite chair, memories of my grandmother played in my mind like a movie projected on a theater screen. Once again, the warm loving energy of Nanny pulsated around me. She explained that I didn't need to call on any relatives for help in the future. She said that I was born with psychic and mediumship abilities that needed to be accepted and developed. Nanny told me I could communicate with all spirits, not just passed-on relatives. She urged me to work with my guides to overcome my fears and embrace mediumship and psychic awareness. She said I had guides in spirit form who would help me with the process. I needed to know and engage them, and they'd help me in embracing my abilities.

"To communicate with spirits is a true gift, Anysia. It is part of who you are in this life." I felt a little scared about embracing my abilities, though she confirmed something I had known my entire life. Nanny said Kathleen was sent to me so I would learn to help others outside my earthly family and to experience one way spirits needed help.

"Sometimes they will need help crossing or they may need a message delivered. There are many ways you will help both those in physical and spirit form," she said. Nanny agreed to help me whenever she could, and I thanked her for being with me in spirit. Feeling her energy once more for that brief time made me realize just how much I missed her. I clasped my hands together attempting to rekindle a lingering impression of Nanny's vibration but she was gone, though only a thought away from me.

I said a final prayer to God and those in the light for helping and protecting me. I sent thoughts of healing and gratitude to Kathleen. I hoped she would heal her soul on the other side, although I thought having the desire to cross over was the first step in her healing process followed by her stepping out of darkness into the light. I thanked her for being part of my first crossing-over experience, which helped me to learn and grow. As I blew out the small white candle, I sent a thought to Nanny, telling her I would do my best to accept my abilities.

SEVEN

Someone Like Me

After crossing Kathleen, the house seemed like a spiritual magnet. The garage in particular attracted lots of energy: lights turned on and off, things fell off shelves, we heard large crashing noises out there, but looked around and found everything intact. There were disturbances inside the house too: the television often turned on by itself, sometimes the volume malfunctioned in the middle of a show, or the sound silenced or blared without any prompting from us. Smoke alarms bellowed regularly without smoke. Baby toys sounded without anyone pressing buttons. At night, the activity continued. Unfamiliar spirits waited in the hallway outside our bedroom. I wasn't sure how they found me, but they came at the same time each night, at 2:30 am—apparently there weren't any clocks in the spirit world. Our dogs ran to the hall, barking and chasing the visitors down the stairs. Brayden would wake up crying either from the barking or just in terror. No one got any sleep at night, and the daytime yielded much of the same activity. This cycle continued for a couple of weeks and affected our entire family.

The dam had broken; spirits flooded every room. I knew there was too much energy in our house, but I didn't know how to control it. I felt constantly wired yet exhausted at the same time. The house buzzed with energy, and we couldn't relax. I remember looking in the mirror one day and touching the circles under my eyes—so dark they looked fake. Brayden was overly tired and cranky. Shane and I argued over silly things, and the dogs could barely keep their eyes open during the day. I had to get the situation under control.

Brayden said something one day that I would've never expected.

"I see kids," he said while pointing his index finger. I didn't question him because I saw them too; they stood in my bathroom doorway and glared at us in my bedroom. At that moment, I realized my little man was just like me. He could see what I could see. I asked him to describe them and he conveyed in detail everything I saw—a little girl in a white dress holding hands with a boy in brown shorts and a green top. They waved at us, and Brayden grinned and waved back at them, saying "hi." The children vanished, but I figured we'd meet them again at some point if we were meant to help them.

The realization that Brayden and I were alike delighted me. I pulled him close and hugged him. He looked up at me with his big brown eyes, and a feeling of responsibility grounded me. My brain flooded with questions. I had to find the meaning in all of this: Why did we have these abilities? Why did the universe send me a spiritually open child? I wondered if Brayden's openness attracted some of this increased energy in our home. More importantly, I questioned how to get a handle on all the energy around us so we wouldn't have constant disturbances.

The answers came one day while I meditated and communicated with my guides. By this time, I knew them quite well and engaged them daily. One of my female guides, Odessa, was considered the gatekeeper. She looked like a middle-aged woman with a medium build and shoulder-length black hair. She wore a long, black cotton dress and flat leather sandals. Odessa's beautiful olive-toned skin complemented her deep-set dark eyes. As gatekeeper, she determined which spirits could get through and which ones couldn't get close to me. But she could only enforce the limits I requested. Since I hadn't requested any limits, she let everyone in. Wasn't that nice of her?

"Couldn't you have just explained how this works? You thought it was a better idea to place the 'Spirits Wanted 24/7' and 'I Love Spirits' signs on my house?" I asked Odessa.

"You're more likely to retain what you learn by experience rather than me telling you things. It's the whole point of being in the physical world—experiencing. You decide what you want in life and your guides lead you to the experiences," Odessa replied.

"Awesome, so at what point did I ask for a house filled with obnoxious spirits?" Odessa laughed a little, though I wasn't trying to amuse her.

"You didn't ask for it, but by not saying it, you're leaving yourself open. This experience is meant to teach you to set limits and decide what you want or don't want." I felt like I was back in one of my undergraduate philosophy classes—twisted in a circular argument that could've lasted for hours. Since I hadn't slept well in a couple of weeks, I knew I couldn't win the argument with a seemingly-omniscient spirit. I conceded.

"Well I can tell you that I don't want a spirit-filled house waking everyone up and creating disturbances all day," I said. Odessa instructed me to write down all the spirit rules I wanted and she would gladly enforce them. I took out a pen, a notebook, and began writing the following:

1. The only spirits allowed in the house are those which had either a family or friend relationship to my husband and me in this lifetime.

2. No one can go to my child to get to me.

3. Anyone being disruptive will be banned.

4. No one can physically impose themselves on the medium.

5. Only I determine when I will help someone—
that person is on my timeline, not the other
way around.

6. I will not seek out complete strangers to deliver
messages.

7. Everyone has to go through the gatekeeper.

8. Waking the family up at night is unacceptable—
they have to come during the day.

I knew other issues would come up, but these rules
seemed like good starting points to establishing some limits
and control. I thanked Odessa for helping me navigate my
abilities.

"I signed on for this duty. You have me for life," she
said, smiling.

"Well I apologize for my sarcasm earlier. I'm irritable
from lack of sleep." I said.

"Don't apologize. I was human, and I understand your
frustration. Plus, you will get it back when you have to guide
me in spirit," she chuckled maniacally like a mad scientist. I
smirked and wondered if she was serious about me guiding
her in the afterlife. I couldn't wrap my head around it, so I
let the thought flow out and said a prayer of gratitude to
my guides and God. After instituting the guidelines with
Odessa, things settled down. An occasional stranger popped
in once in a while, but they usually had a connection to one
of my family members.

I had learned, from my guides, some methods for clearing spirits. One method involved visually tunneling light through every room in the house. It was similar to the method we used to cross Kathleen, except I tunnel light inside the house as well as outside. I also tunneled light inside and out of each member of the household, including the pets. I would do it at night, while resting.

I pictured a tornado of golden light spinning through a room and touching every object and filling it with light. The tunnel extended from the floor to the ceiling. Then I pictured it spinning into every room doing the same thing. I envisioned it ascending the stairs and covering each room on the second floor in light. I sent it up to the attic and down through the crawlspace too. After it spun through all the rooms, I pictured a larger version of it engulfing the whole house in golden light. Then it spun high above the house to the heavens, taking all the energy with it, leaving our home encompassed in golden light. The house had a peaceful energy, and everyone rested soundly. I didn't just use the exercise to clear spirits; I also used it to clear the energy in the house.

Everyone has an energetic imprint. When you have a party, a lot of energy gets imprinted in a house. It is even there if you had a bad day; perhaps someone was angry and there was arguing or stress. All of those things imprint in the home. This clearing technique helps restore balance to the energetic flow.

The toys going off by themselves had scared Brayden. Even though I had a rule with Odessa about not letting anyone into my child's room and had eliminated the problem, I still wanted to do something physical to make him feel safe. Every night, I bubbled him up. I used my hands and outlined an imaginary bubble around his bed. We changed the bubble color each night.

"You're in a protective love bubble. You don't have to worry about anyone bothering you," I would say. Sometimes I gave him a good night kiss after I put the bubble around him.

"Hey, if no one can get in my bubble, then how did you get in to kiss me?" he asked.

"Daddy and I are the only ones who can get in there because we're your parents and love you more than anyone in the world," I replied. He smiled and rested his head on the pillow like a peaceful angel.

Although I knew Brayden had mediumship capabilities, I didn't know to what degree. It wasn't until he mentioned something very specific one day that I actually got an inkling of his awareness capacity. We were in his room reading books, and he walked over to his window and peered out.

Brayden said he saw the sister of one of my cousins. He did not know her name, but he described her with short brown hair wearing a long skirt and a blue top. It sounded like he was describing my cousin who had died of cancer about eight years earlier, but I wasn't sure.

"Where? Is she in our yard?" I asked scanning the yard. I didn't see anyone out there, but Brayden held his gaze out the window.

"She's at her sister's house." The comment startled me— the sister of the cousin passed lived few miles from us in a different town. I really didn't know what he was seeing or how he was viewing it. I continued asking probing questions, wanting to see where we would end up with all of this.

"What's she doing?" I asked.

"She's sitting on a chair, talking about her kids. Her sister is making cookies to bring to my house," he said with a smile. At that point, I realized he must have been seeing my cousin Gail, who had passed. When she died, she left behind her three children. "I like her," he said and looked back at me. His comment didn't surprise me because Gail loved children. I remembered her wedding as a giant party—all the family children were invited. I was about nine years old at the time. At one point, she had all of us on the dance floor in a big circle, holding hands, dancing with her like little fairies circling around a beautiful princess in her stunning white dress and veil. I had a wonderful time and it was one of the only weddings I attended as a child.

About a half hour later, I called my cousin and casually asked her what she had been doing.

"I was making cookies to bring to your house on Sunday," she replied. It was Good Friday, and my cousin was joining us on Sunday for Easter dinner.

"I can't wait to taste those cookies. Did you have a conversation with Gail while baking cookies?" I asked nonchalantly.

"Well, I wouldn't say I was having a conversation because that takes two people, but I was asking her for advice on how to be more involved in her kids' lives," she said. I proceeded to tell her what Brayden shared with me and how he had seen and somehow heard the conversation between them. I didn't know how he could do it, but he remote viewed and heard that incident, all at the young age of three.

My cousin thought it was very cool and didn't seem too shocked. Like most of my cousins, she was open to energy. She knew about my abilities and thought it would be quite natural to have a child just as open as the mother. Brayden's accuracy surprised me a great deal. Not only could he perceive spirits but he also had the ability to somehow transcend space. I honestly didn't know what to do with that information, but I had so many questions. Of course I wanted to know how he could do it, but I was also curious how was he able to see and hear that event. Did my cousin Gail aid the process, so she could provide validation for her sister? Was it a psychic awareness that he could employ at will? Everything Brayden said was so specific, and my cousin validated every detail. Maybe this event was a foreshadowing of things to come. Only time would tell.

Around the same time, Shane needed to visit a Philadelphia museum for one of his college classes. Early one Saturday morning, the three of us ventured to the University of

Pennsylvania's Museum of Archaeology and Anthropology. We took our time perusing the different floors and exhibits. The museum had a mummy exhibit on display, which proved problematic for both Brayden and me. When we entered the space, we encountered various Egyptian artifacts. But as we moved through the darkened exhibit, I sensed intense energy in the space. The room featured glass enclosures which encased mummified bodies of all sorts. I walked over to a mummified family of a mother, father, and young baby. The energy felt unsettled. Brayden walked over to my side and said, "Mommy, that baby should be home. He doesn't like it here." I felt the same way about all the mummified bodies. They weren't at peace. I couldn't stay in that room any longer.

"We'll meet you in the next exhibit." I said to Shane as I picked up Brayden and walked through the doors to the museum's Chinese gallery. After a few moments of viewing jade carvings and other Chinese figures, the intense energy dispersed. I gained deeper insight into Brayden's psychic abilities during that museum visit. I realized I had to find a way to accept and incorporate mediumship and psychic abilities in my life not only for myself but also for my wide-open child. The time of acceptance was at hand; I needed to move beyond the fear and step forward into mediumship. Although, the reason remained a mystery, we had God, angels, spirit guides, family in spirit, and energetic methods to help us along our journey. I trusted that in time, I would know the purpose of mediumship for Brayden and me.

EIGHT

A Greater Purpose

As more spiritual encounters unfolded, I shared them openly with my parents. My father had evolved into a believer since experiencing the spirit in my garage, as well as a host of other encounters. One defining situation involved one of his best friends since childhood, Jack Cashill. Their deep-rooted friendship began on the streets of their hometown in Newark, and carried them through all of life's hurdles.

Jack called my parents' house one day while I was taking care of their dog. They were visiting my sister in San Diego for the first time in seven years. Although she flew back to New Jersey every Christmas, they hadn't been to California since her wedding. When I answered the phone,

I didn't recognize Jack's voice. I mistook him for one of my father's retired firemen buddies. I think Jack expected my mother because he called me by her name. He seemed surprised to know that my parents were on vacation.

"I'm driving to San Diego this afternoon to do some research on my California book," Jack said. "I haven't been to Southern California since your sister's wedding, and I thought it might be nice to take her family out to dinner." He had no knowledge of the fact that my parents were in California as well. I gave him my sister's number. Apparently, Jack and my parents arrived in San Diego within a half hour of each other. He wound up going to breakfast the next morning with her family and my parents.

What were the chances that he and my parents were both in San Diego at the same time and neither of them had been there in over seven years? The chance meeting was pure kismet!

My parents discussed mediumship among other topics with Jack at breakfast, and I honestly don't know all the details. I do know my father explained that we had several family members in law enforcement and had tried discussing the use of mediumship to aid investigations to no avail. We met a lot of skepticism, and rightly so. Even if a medium knew what happened in a missing person case, the investigators needed hard evidence to charge anyone. My father suspected that my abilities had a definite purpose—to help people heal in some way.

I have to admit that I pondered the possibilities of why I was so open to the spirit world, but maybe it hadn't been revealed to me because I had more to learn. Many notable mediums met teachers (other mediums) in their lives who mentored them. My teachers were spirits from the other side. According to my parents, Jack asked engaging questions and seemed very intrigued with my abilities. He wanted me to call him after he returned from California. He had thought of a way my abilities could help someone.

I felt excited to speak with Jack about mediumship. I always enjoyed his visits every summer. He was very intelligent and pragmatic. I remember one time he wore a Maxwell House Coffee cup baseball cap, and I poked fun at him about it.

"What's up with that goofy hat?" I asked in a sarcastic tone.

"I don't care much about fashion," he said with a straight face and continued reading his book.

"Are you serious? What kind of person doesn't care about fashion?" I asked in amazement. I couldn't understand why anyone would wear that hat unless they worked for the company.

Jack shrugged his shoulders without looking up from his book. He certainly threw me for a loop; I had never met anyone like him. Ironically, when Jack and I spoke after he returned, I detected a little bit of uncertainty in his cautious tone, even though he had known me my entire life. I didn't take it personally; it came with the territory. There were lots of charlatans and self-proclaimed mediums and psychics in the world and no one liked being hoodwinked. It took years for most of my immediate family members to believe me. People further from the inner circle were more cautious, and I learned to understand and respect their boundaries.

Jack reiterated some of my parent's dinner discussion. I elaborated on a few details, and he seemed to be taking it all in, saying very little. I explained that I struggled with the purpose of my abilities. Jack thought communicating with a spirit would certainly console bereaved loved ones. He suggested that I reach out to a man named Ron Brown. Besides being my father's best friend and an integral member of our family, Jack was also a well-known author of politically oriented nonfiction. Jack had written a biography of Ron Brown's life called *Ron Brown's Body*. I'm embarrassed to admit my political ineptitude in having not known of Ron Brown, the former Secretary of Commerce who served during President Bill Clinton's first term. As I was about to learn, he was killed in 1996 along with 34 other people, when his plane crashed into a Croatian mountainside. While writing the book, Jack consulted about details with Ms. Nolanda Butler Hill, Ron Brown's former lover and confidante. Jack said she struggled with Ron's loss. The timing seemed impeccable, as the ten-year anniversary of Ron Brown's physical death had just passed. Jack believed that hearing from Ron would bring Nolanda closure and peace.

I asked for Ron Brown's birth name and death date. I explained that I needed the information to ensure I contacted the right person. With a name like Ron Brown, there could have been hundreds of them on the other side. The last name Brown was as common as Smith.

"Yes, of course, I understand what you mean," Jack said. I suspected he was humoring me, playing along out of courtesy to my father. I wasn't offended because as I mentioned earlier, skepticism came with the territory. Let's face it—talking to dead people is weird! If you can see spirits and talk to them, people think you must be a schizophrenic. Actually, the earthly perception of talking to physically dead people is the weird part. We all have the ability to send thoughts with our minds. Have you ever thought of a friend and a day later you get a call from them? Sending thoughts to physically dead family members and loved ones is quite natural, though we've convinced ourselves it's unnatural. I wasn't trying to convince Jack of anything. The accuracy of the information would fill that gap. I knew that when the time was right for Jack, he would come to his own understanding of the afterlife. Whether it was through a message from Ron Brown or someone else was not up to me.

I told Jack I would call him after I spoke to Ron. Then I sat quietly and focused on my breath. I breathed in and out as I closed my eyes. I placed my hands on my abdomen and felt them rise and fall rhythmically with each breath. I settled my thoughts and connected to Ron Brown with my mind. Within a few seconds, yellow lights flickered before my eyes, indicating the presence of energy coming through. A gentle rippling energy vibrated the left side of my body, and I heard Ron's voice. I tried to introduce myself, but he already knew my name. Spirits always know when someone is going to reach out to them. Information exists without limits in the afterlife.

Ron appreciated the work Jack had done to honor his memory. He shared some personal details about himself and his life. Ron loved the taste and smooth texture of red-labeled scotch whiskey. He credited Nolanda as his true life partner not only in business but also as a loving companion. He called her his true love because she accepted him, regardless of his flaws, noting that he had many of them.

Ron mentioned his insecurity that surfaced whenever he spoke. He would say something and then chuckle—a little bit of nervous laughter he inserted into every conversation. Ron said Nolanda tried to help him overcome this nervousness because it could be perceived as a flaw or even perhaps rude if included in the wrong dialogue. He thanked Nolanda for loving him unconditionally and said they shared an eternal connection. I noticed his warm, loving tone when he spoke of her. Before Ron disconnected, I thanked him for sharing his information with me and assured him that I would relay it to Jack for Nolanda. Then I felt his energy pull away, and the yellow flickering lights disappeared.

I sent Jack an email with the shared information and asked him to give me call about the details. He dialed me right away.

"I expected you to say that Ron Brown sends his greetings and well wishes," Jack said with a laugh. We discussed the specifics while Jack jotted down some notes. Although he could not confirm any of the information, he said he would discuss it with Nolanda. A day or so later, Jack called and confessed his utter amazement that Nolanda had confirmed all the details.

"I wrote a book about Ron Brown and I didn't know about his nervous chuckle or his drink of choice," he said in astonishment.

"The information means nothing to me. I'm a neutral party acting as a conduit between two places," I said. Jack said Ron's messages comforted Nolanda. He had an abrupt passing, and it reassured her to know that he came though with so much loving energy. Although I didn't speak directly with Nolanda at the time, Jack forwarded me an email she sent him; as I read it, I wiped a tear from my eye—such beautiful words from a complete stranger. I hoped we would one day speak and perhaps meet in person.

Nolanda and I eventually spoke several times. While I was writing this book, her only son, Andrew, passed suddenly at the young age of thirty-one. His witty, charismatic spirit came through with strength and validation for his mother. Once again, Nolanda received healing from those connected to her on the other side. I thanked Jack for linking us together as both experiences demonstrated how medium-ship could help people heal their hearts. I had a feeling my work with Jack was incomplete, although I was not prepared for what happened next.

About six months later, while working in my home office, I heard a Beach Boys song, "Sloop John B," playing repeatedly in my mind. I recognized this musical method as a way spirits got my attention. John Budney used it all the time with Frank Sinatra's "My Way." I sat quietly, closed my eyes, inhaled a few deep breaths, and asked who was trying to reach me.

A man's voice came through and said he was Jack's father, Bill Cashill. Heaviness enveloped me like a fifty-pound weight on my chest. I asked him to step back a little bit and I breathed easier. I knew Mr. Cashill had died when Jack was in high school, but I didn't know anything else about it. He explained the circumstances involved in his passing. Mr. Cashill had been a Newark police detective. A political shake-up—the Italians had taken power from the Irish—resulted in his demotion to patrolman. The reduction of both title and pay affected his self-esteem and his family's lifestyle.

Depressed and despairing, Mr. Cashill took his own life. I didn't know that aspect of his passing; deep sadness filled my heart and tears welled in my eyes as I connected with his sadness. He said he watched as his wife entered the room and discovered his lifeless body on the bed. Mr. Cashill witnessed the hurt his family endured in his passing and wished he could turn back time. He apologized for his untimely death, which scarred his family and abandoned them. I thanked him for communicating his information to me and promised to get it to Jack.

When he detached, the residual heaviness subsided. I sat for a moment in silence while contemplating the responsibility of sharing this type of information. I recognized that relaying the information could not only bring healing to a spirit in the afterlife but to his family on earth as well.

I sent Jack an email and asked him to call me when he had some free time. I picked at my cuticles as I considered the best way to tell Jack his dad came through. I didn't know how he felt about his dad, and I certainly didn't want to upset him. On the other hand, I had an obligation to deliver Mr. Cashill's information. When Jack called back, we chatted about family stuff. Then he asked, "What's up?" My stomach churned and I inhaled deeply.

"Your dad visited me today," I blurted out. There was silence on the other end of the phone. "I didn't reach out to him and I would never do anything to invade your privacy," I said quickly. My heart raced as I waited for Jack's response, as I knew he would never inquire about personal stuff.

"I'm okay with it. What did he say?" Jack asked. Relieved by his response, I sat back in my chair and told him that based on the place his father was coming from, he did, in fact, commit suicide.

Jack surprised me by laughing. I suppose he sensed my confusion by my sudden silence. He quickly explained, "Hey, if my father didn't kill himself, my mother did, and that's a whole 'nother can of worms."

I shared the details of his father's death—the weapon, the room, the time, the motive. Jack didn't say much except for the insertion of "yes" or "uh-uh" here and there.

"He told me the 'guineas' were just too corrupt," I said tentatively, being part Italian myself.

"Did he use that word?" Jack laughed. "He had to have been pretty upset. The maddest he ever got at me was when I used that word in front of one of his Italian friends."

At the end of the conversation, he elaborated on the facts surrounding his father's death. He asked if my father had discussed Mr. Cashill's passing with me. I told him that we had never discussed it. The only thing I knew was that Mr. Cashill died when Jack was in high school. He seemed surprised by the specifics his father relayed as well as the unexpected visit.

"No one outside our immediate family knew those details," he said, "and there are a few I did not know, although they make perfect sense." A few things Mr. Cashill mentioned eased Jack's mind. No one was in the room when he took his own life, and no one knew exactly why he did it. His message was not only validating but also insightful. Jack realized how truly distraught his father was over the demotion and understood how much his father loved him even in the afterlife.

Jack shared the information with his older brother, Bill. They reviewed the lyrics of "Sloop John B." It had many connections to Mr. Cashill's life, like "the Nassau Town" reference in that the Cashill family first rooted in Princeton, "Old Nassau." The refrain, about wanting to go home, was particularly significant because Mr. Cashill was in a healing place and had yet to go home. The forgiveness of his family would help him get *home*.

I learned a great deal from Mr. Cashill. Although he had passed more than forty-five earthly years earlier, he remained in a place of healing. Linear time had no meaning where he now was. Mr. Cashill was able to speak for himself, though most newer suicide victims did not share the same ability. They sent a messenger to speak on their behalf. He also explained that people on the Earth needed to reach out to suicide victims to get them to the healing place. In most cases, prior to suicide, they had blocked out their loved ones and guides. Once they took their physical lives, they got stuck in the moment and could stay there for a long time if no one reached out to them.

I thanked Mr. Cashill for teaching me about the afterlife of suicides. We left the door open; he could come through as needed. I didn't know if I would see or hear from him again, but I recognized the enlightening information he shared as remarkably hopeful for anyone who has experienced the suicide of a loved one. In gratitude, I sent him thoughts of love, light, and eternal healing. I also thanked Jack for providing these opportunities, which helped me learn and grow. I told him to let me know if he needed my help in the future. Although I still didn't know exactly what to do with mediumship, Jack's experiences had brought me one step closer to that purpose.

NINE

Ask and You Shall Receive

Shortly after Mr. Cashill's visit, Jack's older brother, Bill, was diagnosed with an autoimmune disease. I remember the sadness in Jack's tone when he told me about it. I knew it must have been very hard news to hear, especially since his older brother was like a father to him. I wondered if the timing of Mr. Cashill's visit was somehow connected to Bill's illness. Did Mr. Cashill know Bill would become ill? I couldn't tell without asking him, but I had a hunch that I would know the answer in time.

Jack spent a lot of quality time with Bill during his illness, discussing their childhood, thoughts about the afterlife, and everything in between. I recall Jack saying that his brother was in a good place because of his deeply rooted faith. Eventually, Bill's autoimmune disease led to an advanced type of leukemia. After a courageous battle of two years and a bone marrow transplant, Bill Cashill passed in November of 2009.

Jack sent an email with Bill's funeral arrangements and asked me to keep my eyes open. I felt sadness for Jack and his family; I couldn't imagine losing one of my siblings. I wondered how I would know Bill if he came through because I had never met him. I didn't have any tangible details of him: I had no idea what he looked like, didn't know the sound of his voice or any scents associated with him.

A day later, while at my yoga class, I received an unexpected visit from Bill. At the end of every class, the instructor turned off the lights and took the class through a candlelit, guided relaxation. On this particular night, as soon as the instructor turned off the lights, I saw Bill standing there—a tall man, around six-one, graying hair cut close to his head, with a medium build. To his left was Mrs. Cashill, his mother and to his right was Mr. Cashill, his father—grinning. Mr. Cashill's left hand was around Bill's shoulder's embracing him and his right hand was on Bill's right hand. Mr. Cashill seemed so happy to be reunited with his son, which was evident not only in his warm embrace but also in his beaming smile. Bill said he had always prayed for his father. His mother appeared pleased to have him with her as seen in her facial expression—warmth in her eyes and a faint smile—although she struck me as a little more guarded with her emotions than her husband.

Bill explained that he contracted some type of infection that kicked his disease into high gear. He said that his body was so weak at the end that he knew it was time to leave it behind him. I loved his personality and wished I had met him while he was on earth. He seemed very comfortable in his own skin. Bill had a certain confidence, not to be mistaken for arrogance. It was a quality honed over time with age, experience, and wisdom. His soothing yet assertive voice gave me the impression that he was the type of person to get things done in a calm, controlled way—a leader by example, not by force.

Bill told me Jack would be eulogizing him at the funeral. He said some very specific things he wanted Jack to note in the eulogy. The first thing was that he wanted to stand next to Jack and scan the people in the church and say, "Gee, do you believe I pulled in this kind of crowd? And everybody thought *you* were the family celebrity! Looks like I gave you a run for your money." Bill also mentioned that he wanted Jack to know that there is nothing to fear. He said, "It really is that beautiful; it's truly amazing." Apparently, Jack and Bill had discussed the afterlife before Bill's passing, and his words confirmed their theories. I asked Bill how he found me despite our never having met.

"I can be anywhere at any time," Bill said. Hearing this confirmed information from other spirits about transcending space and time. Bill also noted that he would always be connected to his family even after his physical life ceased. As a result of this eternal connection, he knew when they needed something.

"Jack sends out a thought that he wants me to tell you that I'm okay. Jack thinks it, and I'm here—we are always connected," Bill said. One of the last things he said was that if Jack talked out loud to him, Bill would hear him and would give Jack a sign. Apparently, before Bill's passing, he had promised to send Jack a sign to let him know he was okay.

Bill raised both arms and embraced his parents. Then they were gone. The yoga instructor turned on the lights and I quickly wiped my tears away with my fingertips. I always get teary-eyed during spirit visits because the place where they reside is pure love. When they connect with me, I physically cannot contain so much loving energy and it just spills out of my eyes in tears of joy—the most beautiful feeling.

That night, I emailed Jack all the information Bill conveyed. Jack was gratified and immediately forwarded it to the rest of his family, copying me on the email. He gave very specific instructions.

"Do not share this text with anyone. ANYONE. I would hate to see it on Facebook, but feel free to talk about it," Jack said. He then called me and discussed Bill's words in detail. He explained that it was Bill's wish that he do the eulogy, though Jack's brother Bob was older than he. Jack mentioned feeling slightly uncomfortable passing over

Bob, but Bill had wanted it that way. He also agreed to honor Bill's wishes and incorporate the information I had shared with him into the eulogy. As I hung up the phone, I eased back into Nanny's blue recliner in my office. I tilted my head back and glanced at the ceiling. For the first time in my life, I felt comfortable in my own skin. I was beginning to see why I was able to communicate with spirits.

We drove up to the viewing the day after Thanksgiving. Although the funeral was in New Jersey, it took almost three hours to get there. My in-laws were on vacation and my parents were attending the viewing and funeral, so we brought our children, Brayden and Briella. Brayden was seven at the time and Briella was just over one, which made the car ride a bit of a challenge. I think I sang "The Itsy-Bitsy Spider" and "Wheels on the Bus" at least a hundred times. Fortunately, Brayden watched a movie with headphones and Shane listened to the radio, so they were spared my monotonous singing.

Jack introduced us to all his siblings, nieces, and nephews. I sat with Joan, Jack's wife. We talked about their daughter's wedding, which had been two weeks prior to Bill's passing and she shared wedding photos on her iPod. We could not spend the night to attend the funeral the next day; it was too much for the kids, especially Briella. Toward the end of the viewing, she went into tornado mode—pushing over chairs and shouting. That was our cue to exit and get her to a restaurant as soon as possible so she could have some dinner.

Although we missed Jack's eulogy, I heard about it from my parents. My mother described it as wonderful, and my father said it was the best one he had ever heard, which was a huge compliment since he attended funerals on a regular basis for other firemen as well as police officers. A few days after the funeral, Jack emailed me a copy of the eulogy. It was beautifully written, encompassing details of Bill's childhood right up to his passing. It depicted a wise, well-rounded, loving, elder brother and after reading it, I felt like I knew Bill. Jack used some of Bill's afterlife message in the eulogy:

> *In the last third of his life, Billy learned to appreciate his faith. There is no wisdom without it. This is something that he wanted you all to know and remember, especially his family. And now that he has had first hand experience with what happens next, he would want me to share with you one final thought: there is indeed life after death, and it is a beautiful and amazing thing.*
>
> —Jack Cashill, *Eulogy for Bill Cashill 1941–2009*. November 28, 2009.

When Jack emailed me the eulogy, he sent a note saying, "Thank you for your words of wisdom. You will see how I incorporated them in the eulogy."

"I cannot take credit for the words. They are Bill's, not mine; I'm just the messenger," I replied.

A few weeks after the funeral, Jack emailed me with a question. He said that he awoke to a crashing noise early one December morning. He went downstairs and found that a 25-pound barbell had fallen off the radiator (where it had sat in peace for the last ten years) and crushed a gift bag of tea cups. One other important detail was that the occurrence took place on the morning of Jack's birthday at the very hour of Jack's birth.

"Whaddaya think?" Jack asked. As I read the email, I wondered if Jack's question was meant to be rhetorical. Just then, I heard Bill come through. He said that he knew he could come to Jack because he was open. Bill also knew it was his little brother's birthday, plus Jack had asked him to. I was confused by the last part of what Bill said. What Jack did not share in his email was the fact he asked Bill that morning to send him a sign. Bill confirmed that he not only heard his brother's special birthday request but he also fulfilled it.

"Ask and you shall receive," I said to Jack over the phone. "You don't need to ask me because you already know the answer. You knew it this morning because you asked him for it. Don't dismiss visits as coincidences." Jack chuckled a little. I reminded Jack that Bill is still a living spirit and cannot communicate the way he used to, so he has to find ways that are tangible enough for Jack to understand. A sign like that was hard to overlook and dismiss. "Consider it a special birthday gift," I said.

On Christmas Eve, Jack sent me a copy of an article he wrote for his column entitled *Yes, Virginia, There is Life After Death*. It was the story of his experience and how it not only reinforced his faith but also opened him to a new type of relationship with Bill. I knew the two brothers were on their way to a continuing relationship. As I watched Jack transform from a skeptic to a medium in his own right, I wondered what the future would hold for others like Jack.

TEN

Where I Belong

I struggled with my religion, but not with my faith—there's a difference. The Catholic religion didn't have a place for mediums. Many of my own Catholic family members and family friends really believed that only Jesus and the saints could talk to spirits. A couple of family members actually said right in front of me that mediumship was the work of the devil. Last time I checked, the devil didn't work to help ease grief for bereaved loved ones, but I wasn't an expert, since I had never actually *met* the devil.

My connection with God transcended all aspects of my life. I communicated daily in loving gratitude. I found God everywhere—in the calls of songbirds, in colorful butterflies flittering in the air, through the ocean waves pounding the sandy surf, in the soft rippling wind that rustled my hair, and through the innocent bright eyes of my children. I believed a part of God was in each one of us and in all living things, as a result we were all connected—part of the whole. I never felt disconnected from God. But I felt like I didn't fit into the cookie cutter of Catholicism.

The issue came into focus as Brayden started Catholic school. As a product of the Catholic educational system for primary, secondary, and undergraduate college, I believed in incorporating religious education into the core curriculum. Brayden was a medium, and I knew my daughter would have it too. I recognized the importance of a close relationship with God, especially with our abilities. Catholic school helped build that relationship for me, and the religion reinforced it. I wanted the combination of both for my children, but rejection by the members and the tradition left me jaded. At the same time, the thought of my children growing up without any sense of religion seemed irresponsible on my part. If they decided to make the switch to a different faith in adulthood, they could. But they need some foundation on which to base that choice, if and when the time came. I encountered a crossroads and didn't know which path to take.

I prayed to the Blessed Mother for guidance, as I always viewed her as my real mother, someone I could call on in times of need. Eventually, I realized that I needed to speak to someone in the church. I thought about going to my own church, which I had gone to my whole life, but I felt scared: I hadn't been to church in more than two years as a result of the ridicule about my abilities I received from other Catholics. If I had a dollar for every time someone said it was the work of the devil or evil, or against the faith, I would have been swimming in money. I wondered if the priest wouldn't meet with me for being a nonactive parishioner. I was also really afraid of being judged, rejected, and possibly excommunicated.

My parents had met an elderly healing priest in northern New Jersey, and attended his monthly healing masses. They suggested I give him a call, because he was also known to channel Jesus. I had my apprehensions; in general, older clergy members tended to be more stringent in their views of the church. My parents raved about him, though, and he had mediumship abilities so I figured I'd give him a try.

I mustered the courage and called him one day. I explained that I wanted to talk to someone in the church about my mediumship abilities. He asked me to define "mediumship abilities," so I clarified them as communicating with spirits of those who had passed.

"Well that's definitely against the Church—conjuring spirits is unacceptable in the Catholic church." I thought I might be sick; I realized I had made a terrible mistake. Why had I called this guy? He went on to say that unless it was the "gift of prophecy," the Church saw it as unacceptable. He used himself as an example, and went on to further explain "the gift of prophecy." I inserted a few affirmative comments to let him know I was still listening, while I thought of a way to end the conversation politely.

"But you're not talking about prophecy because you're communicating with spirits other than God, right?"

"Yes, that's correct; mostly it's passed-on loved ones and friends."

"Well, maybe you need an exorcism. I'm in charge of exorcisms for the diocese."

I sat down in a chair and waited for him to laugh, thinking that he was joking. After a moment of silence, I realized his seriousness and misinterpretation of the entire conversation. My face burned with heat, and I clenched my teeth for a moment before taking in a deep breath, releasing the pent-up frustration.

"I'm sure I don't need an exorcism. The devil doesn't want us to help grieving family members, right?" I asked rhetorically.

"Well he is a well-known manipulator. Why don't I send you some information about the 'gift of prophecy' and also exorcisms just in case," he said. I agreed because it was an opportunity to end a pointless call. So I spelled my name for him and gave him my address. I thanked him for his time and his effort to "help" me. Privately, I truly believed *he* needed help in stepping outside his confining beliefs so he could see the missed potential in those around him.

I cried a little as I hung up the phone. I wondered how many other people had traveled down my path, leaving the Catholic church because they were rejected for being different. How many other people were misunderstood and joined other religions or had abandoned the concept of religion altogether? In my opinion, the Church trimmed many too rosebuds before they blossomed. Think of how the beauty of those roses could have enhanced the church. What if Jesus had planted those roses for a specific purpose? Would he be upset knowing someone cut them before they had a chance to flourish?

I needed to have answers to these questions. One down and a full clergy to go, I called my local parish office and left a voicemail for a priest requesting a meeting. When he called back, I said I was struggling with my religion and wanted to discuss it with him. He set a convenient date and time to meet at his office.

The day of the meeting, I heard a Bruce Springsteen song over and over in my head. Though from New Jersey, I'm not an avid fan. I like his music, but I don't listen to often. The song "If I Should Fall Behind" haunted me that day. I didn't know who it was connected to, but it played like a broken record for hours in my mind.

My stomach knotted, when I pulled into the parking lot. Since I had not been to church in such a long time, I didn't know anything about this priest. As I sat on the wooden bench in the waiting area of the office, I prayed silently:

Dear God,

Please help this priest understand me. I want my children to grow up in this religion without feeling rejected. Please help him to be open and understanding. Most of all, thanks for being with me today, because I feel a little scared.

A few moments later, a priest with graying black curly hair greeted me, and I followed him back to his office. He took his seat behind a large cherrywood desk. A chair adjacent to his desk faced the side wall. I sat awkwardly in it for a moment and realized I had to turn my head to see him. I asked to move to another chair that faced his desk, and he of course agreed. I eased into the forward-facing chair and noticed a frame on his desk, which contained a picture of him with an orange-and-white striped cat. It seemed fake; the cat was looking directly at the camera, the priest smiling next to him.

"Is that a real picture?" I asked pointing to the frame.

"Yes, everyone always thinks it's funny," he commented and chuckled.

"Well he's very photogenic. Not only is he posing but he is also looking right at the camera—so peculiar," I said. The priest smiled and I noticed the warmth in his eyes.

"He's a very special cat," he said. Just then, a small black cat in spirit poked his head around the corner of the desk and sauntered toward me. He coiled around my feet and then went back behind the desk.

"Does he come to work with you?" I asked.

"Not so much. I used to take him here often, but now he stays home and sleeps most of the time," he replied. "So how can I help you today?" he asked in a pleasant tone. I leaned forward and explained the reason for my visit. He listened quietly with his hands folded on his desk. I explained that I had always been a Catholic and briefly gave an overview of the breadth of my Catholic education and upbringing. I told him I had attended mass regularly up until the last two years. Then I dropped the bomb.

"I can talk to spirits, so can my son, and my daughter will have the same ability as well," I said in one long breath. I watched his eyebrows rise and his fingers formed a pyramid shape, as he leaned closer to me. I sucked in my cheeks and held my breath for a moment. I hoped he wouldn't freak out.

"Tell me more about this, Anysia," he said curiously. His response was better than the last priest, so I figured I'd roll with it. I explained that I'd had the ability since early childhood and I never knew what to do with it. I tried to ignore it my whole life until I realized my son had it as well. I shared the stories about communications with my deceased family members and friends. He reclined in his chair and listened intently while occasionally interjecting questions. Then I mentioned some of the things about Brayden. I told him my guides said Briella would be even more open than Brayden and me.

"You're lucky you got me, because some other priests are not as open to your abilities," he said.

"Yes, I know. I spoke with a priest in his seventies, and he asked me if I needed an exorcism," I said.

He laughed. "That's exactly what I mean; you could easily be misunderstood. What is it you want from the Church?" he asked, leaning forward in his chair.

"I want the Church to accept my family rather than ostracizing us just because we are a little different," I said.

"I believe everyone has the ability to communicate with their loved ones, they just need to know how to do it. We really aren't that different from everyone else."

"Well it's hard to differentiate between those who have the gift and others who are struggling with some type of mental ailment. There isn't a test we can give to determine authenticity," he said. He made a valid point. But I reminded him that Jesus's befriending of people with leprosy should not only serve as a symbol of compassion; it was also an example of how Catholics should accept all people. He nodded his head in agreement.

"I believe that it may be a gift of the Holy Spirit, as it says in the Acts of the Apostles, 'there are many gifts, but the same Spirit, to some is given the gift of discerning spirits.' The Holy Spirit would bestow that ability to a non-clergy person because in the bible, Jesus selects ordinary people to help with his mission. Look at some of his closest friends, his disciples, Lazarus, Mary Magdalene—all ordinary people."

He also shared some of his personal experience with some people he had met who have the gift of mediumship, and expressed his personal belief in people having mediumship abilities. In his assignment prior to coming to my parish, he had walked with people through many tragic losses, particularly a number of families who lost loved ones on September 11, 2001, in the World Trade Center; he actually accompanied some of them on visits to a medium. My tension eased, and I relaxed back in my seat, knowing he not only understood my abilities but also appreciated them.

He had also lost some young family members and believed they might try to come through at some point. He prayed to them often and said he spoke out loud to them as if they were standing next to him. Then he said something that kind of irked me.

"I had a nephew who died recently, and I was wondering if you had seen him or had any information about him," he said as he looked away from me and focused on his feet. I couldn't believe my ears. He was testing me—a priest—of all people. One priest wanted to give me an exorcism, and the other one thought I was a circus act—the bearded lady at the fair. I wanted to leave, but I remembered that I was there for not only for myself but also for my children. I bit my tongue and thought about it for a moment. I hadn't seen or spoken with any spirits that day, but perhaps the Bruce Springsteen song pertained to him.

"No, I haven't seen him, but I can tell you that I heard this Bruce Springsteen song in my head all morning. I assume it's connected to you because sometimes spirits play music to get my attention. I've never heard that song so many times until this morning."

His eyes glassed as he placed his right hand over his mouth. My heart raced, while I awaited his response, but he sat in silence for what seemed like a couple of minutes. *Great*, I thought. *I made a priest cry—hello excommunication from the Catholic church!* I came to try to work things out with the church, not get kicked out.

He asked me to turn around and look at the picture on the wall behind me. As I turned around, I saw a picture of him with Bruce Springsteen and another man.

"How do you know Bruce?"

"He's a good friend of mine. He sang at my nephew's funeral."

Tears slid down my cheeks, and I silently thanked God for being with me and helping the priest understand.

"When the secretary told me you were here, I said a prayer to Jesus, asking for a sign to let me know you had a legitimate ability. I'm sorry I tested you, but though I am a priest, I'm also human."

I let the frustration dissipate because I completely understood him. He was right. Priests are people too, and they're human, though we sometimes hold them to higher-than-human expectations.

"I'm used to it. There's a doubting Thomas in all of us, right?"

He smirked and nodded his head. "You didn't know about my relationship with Bruce?"

"I haven't been to church in two years. But I think it's totally cool that Bruce sang at your nephew's funeral."

He leaned back in his chair with his hands clasped comfortably behind his head.

"It's a great song. I think I have it in my music library on my computer."

"The lyrics are perfect; I can see why he chose it."

I wasn't sure why his nephew sent the song rather than speaking directly to me like other spirits. But later, the priest explained that his nephew had taken his own life. I had heard from Mr. Cashill—Jack's father, and also my first suicide—that people who committed suicide could not speak for themselves. The priest's nephew had confirmed that fact for me once again.

"So what do you think you will do with this wonderful ability?" he asked.

"That's the ongoing question." I said. I explained that I wanted to use the ability to help others heal not only through grief but also in their hearts. I wanted to help guide people out of the darkness and back into the light. I had no idea how that would manifest.

"If you continue to pray to Jesus, he will lead you to the purpose," he said. I agreed to continue the prayers and asked the priest to keep me in his prayers. It's always good to have a priest saying prayers for you. He smiled and said he would pray for me, as well.

I felt an interesting connection with the priest, like I'd found a lost family member. I told him this and he said the same of me. I explained that before the meeting, I thought he might have kicked me out of the Church. On the contrary, he said that I should stay to help other people learn about mediumship. He excused himself to use the restroom. In his absence, I said a prayer to Jesus. I thanked him for giving the priest his sign and for also keeping it a secret from me. The fact that the priest received his sign and I knew nothing of it beforehand validated my purpose for being there. I realized that moving my seat made the sign possible. If I stayed in the first seat, adjacent to his desk, I would have seen the picture hanging on the wall. When I moved to the forward-facing seat, the picture was directly behind me—out of my line of vision. We definitely had divine intervention that day. A renewed sense of hope rooted me in the Church.

When the priest returned, he put on his stole and asked if I wanted to have my confession heard. For Catholics, confession is the sacrament in which we confess our sins to a priest. Missing Mass is a considered a mortal sin, and since I had missed Mass repeatedly for about two years, confession was necessary to participate and receive Holy Communion.

"I don't want you to confess anything right yet. But I do want to ask for forgiveness on behalf of the people of the Catholic church for not understanding you and not making you feel welcome."

I felt tears cascading down my cheeks as he placed his hand over the top of my head and said a prayer. A current of electrical energy flowed from his hand and down my spine like a charged battery. I had felt this one time before at the age of seventeen, when I attended Mass in Medjugorje, Herzegovina with Father Jozo Zofko. When father Jozo placed his hand upon the top of my head, an electrical current from my head down to my feet. I felt peaceful and relaxed. I recognized this energy as the sign of a true healer.

"You're a healer. I felt the energy run down from your hand."

He smiled. "It's not really me, but rather the Holy Spirit working through me," he said modestly.

I liked his style. He was a new type of priest; I wished there were more like him. Not only did I feel welcomed, I also felt that someone understood me. Of course I knew it would be a long time before the Church completely recognized things like mediumship, but it meant that maybe by the time my children were grown, they would experience a more open Church.

On of my favorite quotes comes from Harper Lee's *To Kill a Mockingbird.* Atticus Finch tells his daughter Scout, "You never understand a person until you consider things from his point of view…until you crawl into his skin and walk around in it."[1] To, me this priest really listened, and I appreciated the time he took to understand my predicament. I thanked him for accepting the meeting and for his compassion. That Sunday I took my family back to church and have continued ever since.

1. Harper Lee, *To Kill A Mockingbird.* New York: Harper Collins, 1960.

ELEVEN

Another One Like Me

My guides had informed me early on that Briella would have fine-tuned mediumship abilities. Though I got a heads-up, I had no idea when her abilities would awaken. I can't exactly say when she began seeing spirits. But I can determine when she first verbalized seeing a spirit. At a few months before her second birthday, Briella still had only a small amount of sandy brown hair on her head. At birth, she had a ton of black hair, so now she resembled a mini-Uncle Fester from the Addams Family. People often mistook her for a boy, which is one of the reasons I decided to get her ears pierced.

Briella ran around the house like a big girl, helping with everything. She loved to put the clothes in the dryer and take them out as I folded them. She had a pretty extensive vocabulary too, although she was still learning the letter sounds of the alphabet. Even when she pronounced something incorrectly, I could usually understand what she tried to say. My husband labeled me a Briella translator.

Shortly before Briella's second birthday party, my mother and I had a disagreement and I kept my distance for a few days. I don't remember the details but I do recall that she yelled at me over something minor. I left her house feeling very hurt and upset; she had a way of not addressing things when they bothered her. The tension would build, and she would verbally explode for what seemed like no reason. In actuality, the outburst was about little things she'd held onto and not addressed.

I thought my mother was completely wrong, but I had a spirit-world visitor who thought differently. The day after the disagreement, Nanny appeared in my living room. As soon as I saw her, I knew why she had visited.

"I'm not apologizing this time," I said. She smiled and tilted her head a little to the left as if to say, "Come on, Anysia, try to be more understanding." I knew the look on her face—one of disappointment. She always had a way of popping in after my mother and I had a falling-out. No matter what happened, she always chided me verbally or nonverbally. I didn't want to deal with it.

"Why don't you go over to Mom's and pop in there with your disappointed gaze? She's the one that flipped out on me. All I did was walk away." Nanny stood there and didn't say a word.

"I'm not budging on this one. She should apologize for that nasty outburst," I said. She continued with her disappointing glare. I turned away and walked into the kitchen.

The next day, while I was dusting upstairs, Nanny silently appeared in the hallway.

"I'm not ready to talk to her," I said as I dusted past her and descended the stairs. When I reached the bottom of the stairs, I glanced over my shoulder. She was gone. It bothered me a little the way she popped in and out whenever she felt like it. It especially frustrated me that she didn't scold my mother. Why were her expectations higher for me than those for her own daughter? Clearly my mother was the problem.

Later, that same day, Briella woke from her nap and I heard her conversing with someone. I opened the door and found Briella standing in the crib.

"Hi, Mama," she said grinning and waving.

"Hello, love bug. Did you have a good nap?" I asked. She nodded her head and jumped up and down a few times—a skill she had recently mastered.

"Air Nahnee go," she asked. At first, I wasn't quite sure if she said "Nanny" or "Nana." The latter is the name she used to address my mother. I never heard her say Nanny's name before.

"What did you say, sweetie?" I asked.

"Air Nahnee go," she repeated and kept jumping up and down on her crib mattress.

"Are you saying 'Nana' or 'Nanny'?" I asked. She handed me her pink satin blankie.

"Nah-nee, Nah-nee, Nah-nee, Nah-nee," she sang. She ceased jumping and began swaying her body rhythmically to her song's tempo. Although I believed in the possibility of Briella seeing Nanny, I wanted to ensure it wasn't a different spirit in the house saying he or she was Nanny. In a house full of mediums, there are always lots of energetic possibilities. My guide, Odessa, usually did a great job at enforcing my guidelines of only family and friend spirits allowed in the house, but I wanted to make sure.

I lifted Briella out of the crib and handed her a sippy cup of watered-down juice. Then I rummaged through my bedroom searching for a picture of Nanny.

When we redecorated our bedroom a few years earlier, I put my Nanny pictures in the attic. I had a few of them framed on the dressers, but later replaced them with pictures of Brayden. When Nanny first passed, I had a really hard time, and seeing those pictures brought back happy memories. After I realized I could still communicate with her in spirit, I no longer needed the pictures. We created new memories together—spiritual ones.

I climbed the attic stairs on my hunt for the photos, but I couldn't find them among the disorganized mess of boxes and holiday decorations. I remembered I had a picture of my sister's college graduation somewhere in my wallet. I might have been sixteen at the time, and Nanny was in the picture. I carried Briella downstairs and found my wallet on the counter. As Briella played with her kitchen set, I flipped through the wallet's plastic photo holder; but I didn't see it. A few of the transparent pockets held several photos. I often placed new ones over the old ones and some of the pockets were six or seven pictures deep. I removed the piles of pictures and sorted through them swiftly. Finally, I found the picture with Nanny at the very bottom of a pile.

I stared at the small picture a moment—remembering that day. The sky blanketed in gray billows, the cool, damp air settled in our bones—uncharacteristic of a May day in Philadelphia. My immediate family and Nanny were in the picture—all of us much younger. I wore a tangerine and floral print skirt and top and matching shoes from the Gap—so cool—or at least I thought I was at the time. In retrospect, it was kind of ugly. Pops, my grandfather, attended the graduation but was not in the picture; he must have been the person taking it. The nostalgic photo ignited youthful, loving memories of my grandparents, and I felt a big smile grow across my face. I held the picture at Briella's eye level.

"Look at the picture, love bug," I said. She focused on the 2 x 2 square.

"Mommy," she said pointing her index finger at me in the tangerine outfit. I was amazed that she recognized me.

"Very good," I said. "Do you see anyone else in the picture?" I asked.

"Nahnee," she said with her fingertip covering Nanny's head.

"That's right. Nanny's in the picture too," I said. She pointed her out, and there were no other pictures of Nanny in the house; she must have seen her. There was no way she would recognize her without seeing her. Nanny died long before Briella's birth.

"Do you see Nanny sometimes?" I asked.

"Ess. Ah see Nahnee," she said while nodding her head like a little marionette. Nanny had a silent, resilient nature. It didn't surprise me that she would hang out with Briella until I was ready to acknowledge her. Plus, I kind of liked the fact that she had visited her great-granddaughter. I asked Briella if Nanny was her friend, and she replied affirmatively by nodding her head again.

The next afternoon, my mother stopped by with a few clothing items she purchased for the kids. Briella ran right over and gave her a big hug. Brayden was playing at a friend's house. She bought the baby a pink pair of sneakers, which Briella had to put on right away; she loved new shoes. While Briella danced around the den in her new sparkling sneakers, I told my mother that Briella had seen Nanny.

"I'm not surprised," she said. "She probably sees all the relatives, but she's too little to say all of their names." I also noted that Briella had picked out Nanny in a photo. My mother wanted to see the photo. I removed it from my wallet and she held it down for Briella to see. We both knelt beside her.

"Can you tell me who you see in this picture?" she asked.

"Mommy," she said pointing with her chubby little index finger. The she glided her finger to the left and identified Nanny. "Nahnee," she said and glanced back at my mother, smiling coyly.

"Good girl," my mother said as tears welled in her eyes. She reached out and hugged Briella.

"Ah la lou, Nana," Briella said.

"I love you too, Briella," she replied. I felt guilty about the argument with my mother. She made an effort by coming over, so I initiated the apology process.

"I'm sorry for the argument we had," I said, biting my thumbnail. My mother looked up at me.

"Don't be. It was my fault. There has been a lot of tension lately and I've been snappy. I'm going to work on it," she said. I didn't expect her to take the responsibility for the argument; she really surprised me.

"We both need to communicate better with each other," I said. I reached out, embraced her, and she gave me a gentle squeeze. Briella must have felt left out because she reached around our calves and clenched us together like a vise. I chuckled and peered down at her. She looked up at me and beamed a tiny-toothed grin that could have assuredly melted the coldest heart. I relished our warm, loving embrace—three generations of women in the same family. Briella gazed into the hallway and waved her little hand.

"Hi, Nahnee," she said. My mother looked in the direction of Briella's wave.

"Where do you see Nanny?" she asked.

"Dare," Briella said pointing at the hallway. My mother didn't see her, but I did. She wore a white silk dress with a small purple-flowered print—one of her favorites. I remembered it well. She waved to Briella. I blew Nanny a kiss, and she smiled and blew one back to me. She wanted my mother and me to work things out. We had worked it out, so Nanny had completed her task. Now she needed to get back to her regular job in the spirit realm.

"It's nice to know she's around and gets to see all the kids," my mother said and wiped her fingertips under both eyes. I nodded my head in agreement. I sent Nanny a thankful thought for visiting and reuniting my mother and me. I also send her an apologetic thought for being a little flip and stubborn in the process; I know she was just trying to help.

Briella came into awareness at the same time as Brayden—right before her second birthday. It wasn't a coincidence that Nanny had a role in facilitating Briella's awareness. Like my son, my daughter could also see, hear, and communicate with spirits. I vowed to guide her through the journey of mediumship with courage and confidence. I would help her understand her abilities and teach her that she had nothing to fear. Although I still didn't know why I could communicate with the spirits of total strangers or what I was supposed to do with my abilities, having two open children with the same abilities propelled me along my path of discovery.

TWELVE

My Purpose

One night as I sat on the couch, I noticed a strange sensation in my palms—like that of tiny spinning wheels. They exuded a warm undulating energy. I told Shane, and he came over and inspected my palms.

"There's nothing there," he said after careful examination. But when I put my palm on his hand, he said it gave off heat and my hand felt like it was vibrating, though it was perfectly still. I decided to place my hands on my chest and the energy relaxed me so much that the last thing I remembered was Shane waking me to go upstairs to bed.

I wondered what the palm energy thing was all about. I knew it provided comfort and tranquility. At night, I placed my hands on Shane and the kids, and the warm energy soothed them. I found it especially helpful for Brayden when he couldn't sleep. After five minutes of my palms on the top of his head, he'd close his eyes and slip into a deep slumber.

Very shortly after the spinning palms realization, one of our dogs, Timber, tore his anterior cruciate ligament (ACL). The x-ray showed a small tear that wouldn't heal itself. He needed surgery or he'd lose the ability to bend his leg. I scheduled the surgery with the orthopedic surgeon a few weeks out. I knew the recovery would be daunting, and I had hoped we could avoid the surgery. Timber was a big, 70-pound baby. If he had the slightest ailment, he milked it by whimpering and making his big amber eyes droop sadly so he could sit on the couch and cuddle like a lapdog.

Each night for about fifteen minutes, I placed my hands on Timber's knee, as he rested soundly on his pillow. The energy funneled through me, out my hands, and into his furry brown body. On the day of the surgery, we took Timber back to the veterinarian's office. We walked him up and down the stark hall while the surgeon observed him. Timber galloped with a perfect gait, and the surgeon couldn't believe it. He said he couldn't perform the surgery in good conscience because the dog had miraculously healed. I didn't mention the energy transfer from my hands; I didn't quite understand it. We drove home and played ball with Timber; he ran more than he had run in several weeks.

I mentioned the energy in my palms to a cousin, and she noted that my hand chakras were opened. I really didn't know anything about hand chakras. She said that one of our cousins was teaching Reiki, and that I should sign up for a class. I enrolled in a Reiki I class and learned self-healing techniques. My cousin was an excellent teacher and had taught many of my other family members. I remember she kept telling me that the Reiki class and attunement were just formalities for me and that I already knew how to heal. I was happy to have a family member to guide me in the basics of energy healing. On my father's side of the family are thirteen Reiki Masters and many clairvoyants and clairsentients.

By the time I finished my Reiki II certification, I converted one of the bedrooms in my home to an office for energy healing. It had a massage table, crystals in the corners to grid the energy, as well as other things to balance the space and keep it in the light. At first I only worked on family members. My dad hurt his shoulder and wanted to try a session. He said the energy soothed his muscles and during his session, both his parents in spirit visited him. Although he was a little confused by the session because he had never experienced anything like it, he said that he enjoyed the connection with parents, especially hearing from his mother. His shoulder felt much better too.

My mother loved the sessions, saying they were like energetic massages. She also embraced the opportunity to communicate with her passed-on family members. The first time she came for a session, about ten of her relatives (most of whom I had never met) from Nanny's side visited.

It seemed like my mom's maternal relatives were at a big family party on the other side. They came through with collective joy, laughter, and validation for her. Her grandfather sang the melody of an Italian childhood tune that he used to serenade her with when she was a little girl. My mother cried as she hummed the tune out loud and recalled him joyfully singing the song while giving her pony rides on his bouncing knee.

Shane and Brayden let me work on them all the time. Shane always fell asleep, so he never really heard the things I communicated during the session; I figured it was his body's way of processing the energy. I continued studying Reiki and completed my master-level. I also finished graduate school at the same time and started writing short stories and articles about my experiences with my abilities. I wasn't quite sure how writing would merge with my abilities and the healing work, but I trusted the process because I knew I was being guided.

As I continued writing articles, I decided to create a blog that contained personal stories about healing, psychic awareness and mediumship (you can find the address in the About the Author section). When I learned new things, I wrote about them on the blog so others could open to similar experiences. I believed everyone had the potential to heal themselves and communicate with their own family members and loved ones in spirit form. The blog was meant to help facilitate that process of sharing information and helping others grow and learn.

Eventually, non-family members were asking me for healing sessions too. I wasn't comfortable bringing strangers into my home because all of us were exceptionally sensitive to energy, including Shane. He had always been clairsentient, but his clairvoyance opened. I remember the first time he mentioned it to me.

"I looked up from the computer in the office and a little boy ran across the room from the piano to the fireplace. You need to take care of that," he said. I reminded Shane that *he* was the one who saw the boy spirit, so maybe *he* needed to take care of it! Shane chuckled and reiterated that I was the medium of the house; any abilities that opened for him were a result of his environment and not of his own intentions.

Thinking about it, I really didn't have any ideas for an office and didn't want a full-time commitment, as Briella was still a toddler. My mother-in-law worked at a nursing home a couple of miles from our home, and asked her manager if I could use their conference room in the evenings for healing sessions. Her manager agreed, so I began meeting people for sessions.

The place worked well for me time-wise because I only needed it a few times a month. However, it had energetic issues. Many people frequented the space, including employees and family members of the residents. It had a lot of energetic imprints, and sometimes when residents passed on, they stuck around and popped in on my client sessions. As a result, I always arrived at the space an hour before the client to set up and energetically clear the building. I tunneled the room in divine light and tunneled the building inside and out in bright light. Then I sent anything that didn't belong through the top of the tunnel, up to the sky.

As I worked with my clients, I could see everything in their energetic fields. If they had experienced trauma, I could see it and sense where they were storing it in their physical bodies. If they had heard negativity and retained it, I would hear it and convey it. I could basically see, hear, and feel what they saw, felt, and heard. Often they had manifested illnesses and didn't know the root causes. By working in their energies, I could see beyond physical ailments and bring to light the causes of their illnesses, which were always emotional, mental, or spiritual.

In addition, family members and friends in spirit form visited during the healing sessions. I would see them and relay physical attributes they displayed such as hair color, clothing, accessories, or any physical ailments they bore during life on earth. The spirits always conveyed information that was necessary or pertinent to the client's healing. For example, if a client had a loved one who died suddenly, that loved one would visit during the session. This allowed both the client and passed-on loved one to have closure and peace.

Those in spirit always conveyed validating details that meant nothing to me but meant a great deal to my clients. I realized that during these sessions, I was a clear conduit between two spaces—the vehicle through which the healing energy was conducted, and through which spirit information was conveyed. I was never the source. The source of the healing and spiritual energy was divine and full of light.

After I had conducted two years' worth of healing sessions at the nursing home, my mother-in-law retired and I needed a new space of my own. I found one in the heart of town. It was a front office with lots of natural light and a bit of ivy growing across the old building's brick face. It suited my needs, and I decorated it in an angel/garden theme, with the help of my sister-in-law. Inside, the walls were beige with white trim, and I had wicker furniture and lots of green plants that brought life to the space. I felt the healing I provided was on a soul-level, so I named the new company Soul-Centered Healing.

My healing sessions were different because they didn't fall into the category of Reiki or any other modality I had been exposed to. I perceived and helped balance and clear everything in my clients' energy fields, which included any spirit communications they had with loved ones on the other side. I realized that my method of healing was different. It healed on a soul-level, hence the name: Soul-Centered Healing.

I had a client with an ongoing depression issue, as well as a cardiac issue. When I scanned his energy field, there was darkness and heaviness as I got to the heart chakra. I explained to the client that I could only see and perceive information the client allowed. Once I said this, I saw images of the client as a young, five-year-old child, scared, on a bed all curled up in a ball crying. The experience played like a video, and I could see the little child's chest rising up and down with each heaving sob. I heard the child's cries and felt the deep sadness of the experience. When I conveyed this to my client, it struck a chord—tears flowed down his cheeks.

The client had been abused by a family member and recalled that exact incident at that age. I explained that I could see the incident because the imprint of the experience was energetically stored in the heart chakra. Only two people knew of the occurrence—the client and the abuser. The client buried the experience, never even discussing it with a friend, spouse, or family member.

The abuser, who was in spirit form, came through during the session and relayed information about the abuse as well as the root of the issue. The client gained an understanding of the abuser's own childhood, which was a key factor in the cycle of abuse. The acknowledgement and apology of the abuser as well as the forgiveness granted by the client helped heal the wounds for both parties. This experience demonstrated how my abilities could facilitate the healing processes for someone on the Earth plane and simultaneously for a spirit in the spirit world.

That session catalyzed my client's ownership of healing. As a result, the client enrolled in a counseling program with a therapist and learned to heal through the abuse. Ultimately, he resolved his depression and cleared his heart issue. Often people are aware of the experiences they've had in life but they're not always aware of how they correlate to disease in their bodies. Our physical bodies are a culmination of our physical, spiritual, mental, and emotional experiences.

Sometimes the information that came through in sessions was very specific and not always what clients wanted to hear—but it was always information that needed to be heard. Often spirits addressed conflict with their living relatives. It could be outstanding conflict because of a sudden passing or conflict among relatives on the Earth. I had a mother come through and address the sibling rivalry among her adult children. It began after her passing and the distribution of her estate. She wouldn't leave until they agreed to stop fighting.

Spirits do many things to get our attention and let us know they're around, especially during times of our stress. Although they don't have physical bodies, they use signs that cater to our physical senses so they're easier for us to perceive. A spirit's form is comprised of electromagnetic energy, the same type of energy field in our electrical and radio waves. When spirits are around, their energy fields disrupt those electrical and radio waves, resulting in disturbances such as flickering lights, sound not working on the television, or radio stations losing their frequencies.

Spirits can and will move things on the Earth plane. It takes a lot of energy for them to perform these acts, so it's not a regular occurrence, unless they really need to get someone's attention. They may slam doors, move objects off shelves, or knock things over. They can also emit scents like that of a certain perfume, smoke from a pipe, or something food-related that was connected to them when they were alive, recognizable to a loved one or friend. Spirits might relay flavors or tastes, which a medium can communicate to a client. I often get what I call "chemo-nausea," when I'm communicating with a spirit who passed while receiving intense chemotherapy. Chemo-nausea differs from regular nausea because it is accompanied by a horrific metallic taste. I certainly prefer the taste of chocolate or any other sweet flavor over that one!

One of the most amazing things that happened with a client in a session involved a very vibrant spirit. I had a client who reached out to someone in the spirit world. The spirit had been a very flashy dresser—lots of bright colors and feather boas. As I communicated with the spirit at the end of the session with my eyes closed, the client asked me to look down at my hand, which was resting on the table. There in my open palm was a bright yellow, two-inch feather. I had no idea where it came from. The client said the feather had mysteriously appeared on my long black hair, and when I casually touched my head to place in my hair behind my ear, the feather stuck to my hand. There were no feather pillows or any other feather objects in my office; it was physically impossible for it to materialize in my office.

I had experienced spirits moving physical things in a room, but that feather was the first time a spirit produced something physical out of thin air. My client knew it was a sign from the beautiful spirit, and wrapped in a white tissue to take home as a souvenir. I attributed this type of physical manifestation to the spirit's magnificent energy. In life on Earth and in the spirit world, this spirit's energy remained sparkling and vivacious.

Working with my clients has helped me understand how and why I have these abilities. Acting as the conduit between the Earth and spirit planes is helpful to spirits and humans. I'm grateful to the Divine for my abilities, and I'm honored to work with my clients. Each client and experience is different, and I'm always learning and growing. Whatever I learn is shared with others via my writing or in lectures and classes because we all grow collectively by sharing information.

My story demonstrates a process of development. I transformed from a scared, reluctant medium and blossomed into a competent, confident professional guiding my own children through spirit communication as well as those around me.

There were three main components that aided this process: my connection to the Divine, assistance from those in physical and spirit form, and true love and acceptance of myself.

Mediumship and psychic awareness are innate abilities in each of us. We come to the earth wired for spirit communication. As infants we incarnate with soft spots or fontanelles in the skull, one of which is at the top of the head—the location of the crown chakra—our connection to the Divine. When a child's openness is nurtured, he or she retains an unobstructed strong connection with God and the energy in the universe, which includes the spirit realm. Although I didn't grow up in an environment that supported my abilities, I remained open and always deeply connected to God. Perhaps that is an intentional part of my personal process. I might not have written this book and helped others tune in if I had not gone through such a lengthy learning journey.

I never had a spiritual teacher or guru on earth who guided me, but there were many people both in spirit and physical form, who taught me a great deal. When we meet new people, we never know if they'll be in our lives long-term. They float in and out of lives like the ebb and rise of the ocean tide. But if we trust and have faith that God has put the right people in our paths, we can be assured that we'll always have assistance sailing the sea of light with guides both on the Earth plane and in the spirit world.

Mastering self-acceptance took a long time for me; I sought approval from others including family members, friends, and even a religion. But I eventually learned that until I totally and completely approved of myself, I wouldn't gain acceptance from others. As I embraced myself and my abilities, I learned self-acceptance, the only kind of approval I ever needed.

Having children with the same aptitudes forced me to overcome fears and propelled me on my path of purpose for mediumship and psychic awareness. I use my abilities to help others heal. I also teach people to develop their own psychic and mediumship skills. I love the work I'm doing, and I thank God everyday for the colorful, magnificent journey of my life. I can honestly say that "I took the road less traveled by, and that has made all the difference."[2]

The exercises at the end of this book are meant to help people discover their own psychic and mediumship skills. Mediumship takes practice and time, so don't be discouraged if you don't master it at the onset. Allow yourself a learning curve to develop your new abilities—I've had a lifetime to perfect mine. Perhaps not everyone will develop their faculties to the point of communicating with complete strangers. With a little practice, however, everyone can reach a point of communication with the spirits of their passed-on friends and loved ones. Death is really an illusion; only our physical bodies die. Our souls are eternal and life is everlasting.

---

2. Robert Frost, "The Road Not Taken." *Collected Poems of Robert Frost.* New York: Henry Holt and Company, 1939.

THIRTEEN

Mediumship Methods— an Overview

Mediumship is a magnificent ability that allows us to communicate with those in spirit form. There are several ways we can perceive spirit information using our psychic senses. If we do not have all our psychic abilities developed, the information will come through whichever sense or senses are most developed. Hopefully by this point in the book, you have a good idea of how mediums perceive spirits and communicate with them. Chapter 14 defines what a medium is and gives deeper insight into these abilities.

When you first venture into spirit communication, you may want to consider meditation. In order to perceive spirit information, you need to be able to block out things going on in the physical world and commit your attention to the spirit realm, which takes some practice. I have included both a basic meditation as well as an advanced one. Meditation is a valuable tool because it helps us control our thought process, which is essential in spirit communication.

There are exercises listed in this book to help you develop your psychic senses and—eventually—your mediumship abilities as well. The hand-holding exercise helps enhance your clairsentience. The second clairsentience exercise creates more physical distance from your partner, allowing you to increase your clairsentient abilities. The color exercise helps develop clairvoyance and your third eye. The number exercise improves your clairaudience.

There are a few things to know when trying to reach passed-on family and friends. We generally don't communicate verbally with them. The preferred method of communication is telepathic. We send thoughts with our minds and they send thoughts back to us. So for example, if you are communicating with a family member, you may want to tell them that you love and miss them. You would think the thought of loving and missing them in your mind. Once you do this, the thought is sent to them. The family member will receive it and send one back to you. The phone call exercise helps refine this ability.

As you are working on meditation and telepathic communication, you might also want to reach out to your guides. Communication with guides can be helpful for several reasons. It is of course helpful for contacting passed-on family members. Your guides are also with you to help you find your way and complete you life's mission on Earth. They are always there to assist you—all you need to do is engage them. There is an exercise in this book that will assist you in meeting and communicating with your spirit guides.

As you open up to spirit communication, you may find you are a little more emotional. You may become more sensitive to the energy around you. These are natural parts of the process for some people. If at any time you feel uncomfortable, engage your guides. They're there to help, hence the name, "guide."

Whenever we reach out to anyone is spirit, we need to shield our energy. We want to ensure that we only connect with energy in the light. We also want to block out all other energies and only communicate with the spirit we are trying to reach. I list several methods for psychic shielding. You can choose whichever method suits you.

Grounding is a way to keep our energy connected to the earth. As I mentioned earlier in the book, most spirits vibrate at a higher rate than humans. When we communicate with them, two things happen: they lower their vibrations a bit and we raise ours, so we meet somewhere in the middle. After spirit communication, we need to ground ourselves so we don't feel disconnected from our bodies. If we are ungrounded, we may feel dizzy and spacey—like we are floating somewhere in the stratosphere. By grounding ourselves, we stay connected to our bodies and the earth, fully present in our lives.

Now that we know the basics of working with our guides, psychic shielding, and staying grounded, we are ready to communicate with our loved ones in spirit form. There are several ways to connect with our loved ones. We may want to telepathically ask them to send us a specific sign or symbol. If we aren't comfortable asking for a sign, we may want to ask for a dream visit. There are exercises listed for each method. You may choose one over the other, or you may want to try both.

One of the most difficult challenges for parents is losing a child. They often feel like God has singled them out by taking their child, creating many mixed emotions for them. We can communicate with passed-on children the same way we do with adults who have crossed over. We can ask them to visit us in dreams or we can set up a system of signs and symbols with them. Parents first must abandon the longing for a physical connection with a passed-on child. They need to embrace the concept of having a continued spiritual relationship with that child.

The sudden passing of loved ones create voids in our lives. When a loved one passes suddenly, we are robbed of the opportunities to say many things, including a final goodbye. The good news is that there is a way to communicate all those things to our loved ones after they have passed. We can write a letter and read it aloud or telepathically to them. The exercise for this is a simple one, yet it's very effective for bringing closure.

Suicide victims can't readily communicate like other spirits. They need soul healing. Sometimes they may get stuck. Suicide is a dark act shrouded in dark energy. We can reach out to them and help them step into the light. But we need to first engage our guides and psychic shield. Once those who have committed suicide step into the light, they begin the soul healing process. The exercise in this section helps guide those who have committed suicide into the eternal light.

I'm often asked if pets have souls and if they live on in the afterlife. Of course I hold the belief that the souls of pets live on. I have not only received validation from my own pets that have crossed over, but I have also seen pets of deceased people come through client sessions. We can ask our pets to send us signs and symbols or visit us in dreams the same way we would ask any other spirit.

Space clearing is a practice we should engage in regularly—it is not just for clearing space after we communicate with spirits. We also need to clear the space because of the energetic imprints we create daily. If we have a day of stress or anxiety, the imprint of that energy remains in our homes long after we change our state of mind. Just as you physically clean your house regularly, so should you do it energetically. Space clearing is a way to bring balance to our environments.

Like space clearing, cord cutting is another activity we should perform regularly. We form energetic cords regularly with people, places, and situations. When we fail to cut cords, we leave a number of energetic draws open on our energy. This depletes our own energy source.

With a bit of practice and patience, hopefully you'll be on your way to communicating with your loved ones. I've given exercises that cover the basics, including development of your psychic senses, basic mediumship, psychic shielding, grounding, and cord-cutting. Practice each exercise several times until you've mastered it. Once you become proficient at an exercise, move on to the next one.

These exercises are arranged in a specific chronology and should be followed as such. The exercises about contacting your guides, shielding your energies, and grounding should always be employed before reaching out to anyone in spirit to ensure that your energy is protected and unwanted energy is blocked. The space clearing and cord-cutting should always be used after you reach out to anyone in spirit to sever any energetic ties you created and remove any energetic imprints.

At the end of this book is a recommended reading list of books by fellow Llewellyn authors for further reading along your development journey. May you always be held in the Light and eternally connected to your loved ones in spirit.

FOURTEEN

What Is
a Medium?

The concept of mediumship elicits mixed responses in people. Some really understand it, others are cautiously intrigued, and some people blatantly deny the existence of spirits or the fact that the living can perceive and communicate with them.

I have come to realize that in many cases, mediumship makes people uncomfortable because they don't know much about it. For some, mediumship falls into the category of mysterious unknown things hidden behind a dark grey curtain, along with the possible existence of Bigfoot and Nessie.

Certain organizations that involve mediumship have helped provide information and clarification about spirit

communication. Spiritualism is a science, religion, and philosophy of continuous life based on communication with
spirit through mediumship. Spiritism is another science,
religion, and philosophy that also holds the belief in continuous life via spirit communication and mediumship. It
is more scientific than Spiritualism because it has provided
in-depth, extensive research in mediumship, various types
of spirits, and spirit communication.

Mediumship is the ability to communicate with spirits.
All mediums are psychic, meaning they can perceive energy
beyond the physical senses. Mediumship takes psychic ability a step further. Mediums can sense spirit energy, discern
it, and communicate with it. Some mediums are born with
abilities that allow them to communicate with spirits as
early as infancy, which was the case for me and my children.
Other mediums develop their abilities over time.

Mediums use their psychic senses to perceive spirit
energy. Not all mediums use the same senses because not
everyone has developed all psychic senses. For me, mediumship is very natural. I do not enter an altered state to communicate with spirits. I am fully conscious and can receive
information through all my psychic senses. I generally use
the following psychic senses in communicating with spirits:

Clairvoyance ("Clear Seeing")

This is the ability to receive mental images from spirit. With
this ability, I can describe what the spirit looked like physically. Spirits will communicate clairvoyantly by sending pic-

tures of places, objects, or symbols. I perceive these images using my third eye (located in the center of the forehead) rather than my physical eyes. Spirits will often send me visual images of objects they owned in life that are now in the hands of a family member.

Once in a session with a client, a woman in spirit showed two images: One was a beautiful solitary pearl set in a gold ring, which I conveyed to the client. The other was a crystal pendant on a silver chain, which the client wore during the session. The woman in spirit had worn both pieces of jewelry when she was alive. The client held and wore them to feel close to the passed-on woman.

Sometimes I get a visual image of what a person looked like in physical life and I can communicate that to my client. I may also get a visual image of a house, location, other people, and so on that can be shared during a session. In addition, I can often see spirit with my physical eyes, although I am not sure honestly how I can do it. As you know from the first chapter, I have been able to see spirits since childhood, so it is very natural for me.

Clairaudience ("Clear Hearing")

This ability allows one to receive information from the spirit realm without the use of physical ears. This is also referred to as mental telepathy, communication through thoughts. When I use clairaudience with spirits, they communicate information and details about their lives on earth through thought. I may ask additional questions using my mind and the spirits respond through thought as well. I share this with my client as well as any inflection or tone the spirit uses to convey the information. Often, inflection or the way a spirit says something is very important to someone. In a session with a client, her passed-on mother shared information in a sweet whisper that could barely be heard. When I conveyed this to her the woman said that her mother whispered those words to her every night as a child, when she tucked her into bed.

Clairsentience ("Clear Feeling")

Through this ability, I can perceive information and impressions through feelings. I can feel emotions of spirits and clients, as well as environmental factors such as heat or cold, though those things may not physically be present. I can *feel* a method of passing. For example, I may feel tremendous pressure in my chest and then an explosion of energy in the heart. This is a spirit's way of communicating a passing through a heart attack. Sometimes, I feel extreme nausea that I also refer to as chemo-nausea. When I feel this way in a session, I know I'm communicating with someone who received chemotherapy and died as a result of a terminal illness such as cancer. I learned my lesson early on with this ability in the experience with the spirit, Kathleen, in my garage. Sensing a method of passing is not usually a good feeling, so I have learned to keep the physical impressions to a minimum. But feeling the energy of loved ones that have passed is a wonderful experience. I often cry when I feel the energy of someone that was close to me because it is so magnificent to feel that loving energy once more. It makes me realize how much I miss their energies but I am grateful at the same time to be able to connect.

Clairscent ("Clear Smelling")

With this ability I can smell scents without having them physically present. In a session, I will smell a certain perfume or food scent that is connected to a person that has passed. In a session for a friend, a grandmother came through as the smell of sweet peppermint candy tickled my nose. It reminded me of those little red and white swirled hard candies. My friend said his grandmother always had peppermint candies in her pocket for her grandchildren. Sometimes my maternal grandmother, Nanny, visits in spirit form. She carries the scent of Dior Poison—her favorite perfume. I love the scent because I know as soon as I perceive it she's not far behind.

Clairgustance ("Clear Tasting")

With this sense, I can taste substances without putting anything into my mouth. For example, I might taste chocolate during a session. Sometimes I get a strong medicine or metallic taste in my mouth during a session. This lets me know that the person was on some type of medication at the end of life on earth.

Clairtangency ("Clear Touching")

With this ability I can hold an object and pick up any energetic impressions attached to it. This is also know as psychometry. I use this ability the least in my work because it requires having me hold an object that belonged to someone who has passed. Much of what I do as a medium is with my mind. Sometimes a person might bring an object to a session that was owned by someone who passed, but it is not needed.

Spirits may use one or more or all methods to communicate. Some may communicate only through clairaudience and clairvoyance. Others may choose clairvoyance, clairscent, and clairsentience. The decision about which methods are used is actually twofold. If the medium has not developed all his or her abilities, a spirit will choose to send information in the way that is most suitable for that person. If the medium has developed all abilities, then the spirit will send information in whichever way is best suited for the spirit. As spirits evolve on the other side, they are able to send information in a variety of ways, thus with a fully developed medium, a fully developed spirit can send information to all the medium's psychic senses. A newer spirit may only be able to send images or something simple. I prefer clairaudience, clairsentience, and clairvoyance, although depending on their methods of passing, some spirits might not be able to communicate for themselves; they may send signs rather than words.

There are many reasons spirits communicate with us. They often send us signs though we may not always be open to receiving them. I personally feel I am on the Earth plane to help facilitate communication with spirit. I'm also here as a teacher to open the door for others, so those in physical form can take the steps to communicating with their passed-on loves ones. Maybe as people become more comfortable with mediumship over time, they'll release their fears and open to it. Only then will we lift the opaque curtain that hangs over mediumship. In doing so, we'll reveal mediumship and illuminate it as a truly universal tool that enables communication with our friends and loved ones in spirit form.

FIFTEEN

Meditation

There are two meditation exercises listed here. The first is a basic exercise designed to help you connect within as well as ground yourself. The second is a chakra meditation I use to balance my energy on a regular basis. What follows are examples of meditations; you can use any meditation that helps you relax your mind and focus within.

Basic Meditation Exercise
What You Will Need:

> 1. Your mind in a calm state

> 2. A place to sit down or recline

One of the first steps in communicating with our deceased loved ones is to tune out all earthly things around us and tune into our souls. The easiest way to do this is through meditation. If you aren't used to meditation, there are several ways to accomplish it. You can mediate at a designated place such as a church or temple. You can also do it in a comfortable room in your house, or you might want to do it outside, sitting or walking with nature. Choose an environment where your mind can unfold and relax. It may be hard to read the meditation for yourself. You might want to have a friend read it to you as you concentrate on the spoken words of the meditation. Perhaps you can read the meditation for a friend as well.

Close your eyes, and sit quietly for a moment. Allow thoughts to flow through your mind, but don't follow any of them. Just let them bubble up and release into the air. Concentrate on your breathing. Breathe in through your nose and out through your mouth. Try to breathe in to the count of three and out to the count of three. Observe your abdomen rise and fall with each breath. Feel all tension releasing from your body. Notice all the muscles in your face relax. Press your tongue against the roof of your mouth and notice the jaw line relax. You may also open your mouth a little bit and relax all those muscles a bit more.

Feel this peaceful energy as it moves down your ears into your neck. Sense the energy as it loosens all the muscles in your neck and unties all knots. Observe it moving down your arms and unclenching your fingers and joints. Feel it slip down to your chest as it eases all pressure, and breathe freely when it reaches your lungs. Breathe in a few deep breaths and enjoy the cool, crisp air as it fills your lungs and oxygenates all your cells.

Focus your attention on balanced energy floating down into your abdomen. Notice as it massages your organs and digestive track. Feel the energy cover your upper legs. Sense the lengthening of your muscles as this energy soothes each fiber in your legs. Feel it in your knees as it clears out anything, including emotions you are storing there. See it in your calves, loosening the muscles there as it makes its way down to the ankles. Feel it unlocking the joints and opening them. Allow the energy to flow down to your feet. Take note as all soreness and aches leave your feet and dissipate into the earth. Take a moment and enjoy this relaxing energy as it flows throughout your entire body. Your mind and body are one and at peace.

Now that you're relaxed, fill your mind with thoughts of all the people, experiences, and things you're grateful for in your life. You may be grateful for your home, your job, your health, family, friends, and pets. Send thoughts of gratitude to all the people in your life who make you feel happy and loved. Perhaps you want to include pets in here as well because they too help us experience love. Make a mental note of any images that flash before you—some people see colors, abstract images. Take notice of any sounds or nonverbal information you receive at this time.

Next, picture a large golden cord coming down from above you. See it touching the top of your head, illuminating it inside and out in brilliant golden light. Observe this gold brilliance flowing down your body, slowly brightening everything in its path. As this light moves down your body, permeating ever cell, it illuminates your body inside and out in a warm, golden brilliance. When the bright energy reaches your feet, it spills out onto the ground, as you stand in a shallow pool of this liquid gold. Feel the warmth of this new energy in your body. Sit for a few moments basking in this golden light.

Now feel the golden cord disconnecting from the top of your head. Look upward and see it being pulled back into the heavens. Watch the cord dissipate high up into the sky. Focus your energy once again on yourself. As the golden energy continues pulsating through your body, you feel warmed, energized, and loved. Know that this energy is always available to you. Anytime you need to recharge or feel a loving connection, you can pull the cord down and fill yourself with this golden energy.

Imagine another cord—a red one—extending downward from your root chakra (the energy center located just below your pubic bone) to the center of the earth. See this crimson cord as it sinks deep into the bright orange lava floating in the Earth's core. Feel it anchoring you, and like a magnet, it pulls all your energy down from your head to your feet. As your energy moves down your body, you feel heavier. As this heavy energy reaches your feet, you strongly sense the earth's magnetic pull. It draws the energy from your feet down the cord, solidifying your connection with the earth. You are fully present in your body and your energy is heavily grounded. Picture the cord disconnecting from your root chakra and falling all the way down to the earth's center. Watch as it is reabsorbed into the molten lava. You're one with your body, mind, and spirit.

Open your eyes and relax for a moment, collecting your thoughts about the meditation. Write down any questions, information, or images that may have come up in the process. Meditation takes a little time, but you should try to do it once a week to train your mind to disconnect from everything going on around you. It's paramount for spirit communication.

Advanced Chakra Meditation Exercise
What You Will Need:

1. Your mind in a calm state

2. A place to sit down or recline

The word *chakra* (pronounced "sha-kra") comes from the Indian Sanskrit word meaning "wheel" or "spinning disk." Our chakras are the major energy centers dedicated to particular parts of our body and associated with our spiritual advancement. The chakras are generally five inches in diameter and work like power stations for the body. Our bodies are made up of an electromagnetic energy, and the flow of this energy affects our well-being. Each chakra vibrates in a clockwise direction, and is responsible for energizing different vital organs, nerves, and muscles, as well as distributing energies throughout our bodies.

Every human being has seven primary chakras located vertically along the spinal column, running from the base of our spine (between the legs) to the top of our head. There are several other chakras in our energy field, but for the purposes of this meditation, we will work with the primary seven. I label this meditation as advanced because we use some of our psychic senses to scan the chakras. We use our clairvoyance for visualizing the chakras and we use clairsentience to feel the energy.

Before any meditation, whether it is basic or advanced, we want to make sure we're in a relaxed position. This can be sitting up in a chair, reclined, lying completely flat, or whatever is most comfortable for you. We want to close our eyes and concentrate on our breathing. Sometimes it's helpful to place your hands gently on your abdomen and feel it rise and fall with each breath. As your respiration rate slows down, notice all the muscles in your body beginning to relax.

Concentrate only on your breath. Breathe in peace and relaxation. Breathe out any stress, anxiety, and tension. Do this for a few minutes, breathing in relaxation and releasing any stress with each exhale. When you feel you're in a comfortable and relaxed state, you're ready to begin.

First, you want to ground your energy—imagine large, soft brown tree roots growing from the earth and coiling around your feet, extending up your legs. The soft roots pull your energy down and keep you deeply planted. Feel your energy unifying with that of the earth, and sense safety and comfort filling your body. Once you are strongly grounded, you're ready to balance the chakras.

As we scan our chakras, we are checking the shape, size, color, and spin of them. Healthy chakras are perfectly circular in shape. They're the size of our palms. Our chakras are bright vibrant colors. They spin in a clockwise direction. If any chakra points don't display the above listed attributes, they need some balancing to get them back into a healthy state.

Root Chakra

Raise your hands and place them on your pubic bone. Feel the energy of the root chakra. Notice any differences in the fluctuations of the energy. Does it flow freely? Picture the chakra in your third eye as you connect with the energy. Notice the chakra's movement. Is it spinning? Is it moving in a clockwise or counterclockwise direction? What is the chakra's color? Is it a vibrant red? Is it dark, muddled red, or perhaps a shade of red mixed with orange? Take note of the shape. Is the chakra round or oval-shaped? Observe the chakra size. Would it fit nicely in your palm? It is the size of a grapefruit? Is it the size of a peanut?

If you notice anything out of the ordinary, ask your body why an imbalance is there. What is it about? Imagine the chakra healthy, spinning clockwise in a bright red color—a beautiful, vibrant red ball of energy that fits nicely in your palm. Hold your hand on the chakra until you can see it as perfectly healthy.

Keeping one hand on the root chakra, place the other on your second or sacral chakra, located two inches below the navel. Feel the energy moving upward between your hands. Feel the connection between the two chakras. Once you feel this healthy movement upward, you're ready to balance the second chakra.

Sacral Chakra
Place both hands just below your navel. Feel the energy in your second chakra. Notice any differences in the fluctuations of the energy. Does it flow freely? Picture the chakra in your third eye as you connect with the energy. Notice the chakra's movement. Is it spinning? Is it moving in a clockwise or counterclockwise direction? What is the chakra's color? Is it a beautiful bright orange? Is it dark orange, or perhaps a shade of orange mixed with yellow? Take note of the chakra's shape. Is it round or oval-shaped? Observe the chakra size. Would it fit nicely in your palm? It is the size of a grapefruit? Is it the size of a peanut?

If you notice anything out of the ordinary, ask your body why an imbalance is there. What is it about? Imagine the chakra healthy, spinning clockwise in a bright orange color—a beautiful, vibrant orange ball of energy that fits nicely in your palm. Hold your hand on the chakra until you can see it as perfectly healthy.

Keeping one hand on the sacral chakra, place the other on your third or solar plexus chakra, located just above the navel directly center, below the sternum. Feel the energy moving upward between your hands. Sense the connection between the two chakras. Once you feel this healthy movement upward, you are ready to balance the third chakra.

Solar Plexus

Place both hands just below the center of the rib cage. Feel the energy in your third chakra. Notice any differences in the fluctuations of the energy. Does it flow freely? Picture the chakra with your third eye as you connect with the energy. Notice the chakra's movement. Is it spinning? Is it moving in a clockwise or counterclockwise direction? What is the chakra's color? Is it a bright, sunny yellow? Is it muddled yellow, or perhaps a shade of yellow mixed with green? Notice the chakra's shape. Is it round or oval-shaped? Observe the chakra size. Would it fit nicely in your palm? It is the size of a grapefruit? Is it the size of a peanut?

If you notice anything out of the ordinary, ask your body why there is an imbalance. What is it about? Imagine the chakra healthy, spinning clockwise in a bright yellow color—a beautiful, vibrant yellow ball of energy that fits perfectly in the palm of your hand.

Hold your hand on the chakra until you can see it as healthy. Keeping one hand on the solar plexus chakra, place the other on your fourth or heart chakra, located directly in the center of your chest. Feel the energy moving upward between your hands. Sense the connection between the two chakras. Once you feel this healthy movement upward, you're ready to balance the fourth chakra.

Heart Chakra

Place both hands on your heart center. Feel the energy in your fourth chakra. Notice any differences in the fluctuations of the energy. Does it flow freely? Picture the chakra in your third eye as you connect with the energy. Notice its movement. Is it spinning? Is it moving in a clockwise or counterclockwise direction? What is the chakra's color? Is it a bright green? Is it dark green, or perhaps a shade of blue mixed with green? Notice the chakra's shape. Is it round or oval-shaped? Observe the chakra size. Would it fit nicely in your palm? It is the size of a grapefruit? Is it the size of a peanut?

If you notice anything out of the ordinary, ask your body why there is an imbalance. What is it about? Imagine the chakra healthy, spinning clockwise in a bright green color—a beautiful, vibrant green ball that fits in the palm of your hand. Hold your hand on the chakra until you can see it as healthy. Keeping one hand on the heart center chakra place the other on your fifth chakra. Feel the energy moving upward between your hands. Feel the connection between the two chakras. Once you feel this healthy movement upward, you are ready to balance the fifth chakra.

Throat Chakra

Place both hands on your throat. Feel the energy in your fifth chakra. Notice any differences in the fluctuations of the energy. Does it flow freely? Picture the chakra with your third eye as you connect with the energy. Notice its movement. Is it spinning? Is it moving in a clockwise or counterclockwise direction? What is the color? Is it a beautiful crystal blue? Is it aqua or perhaps a shade of blue mixed with any other color? Notice the chakra's shape. Is it round or oval-shaped? Observe the chakra size. Would it fit nicely in your palm? It is the size of a grapefruit? Is it the size of a peanut?

If you notice anything out of the ordinary, ask your body why there is an imbalance. What is it about? Imagine the chakra healthy, spinning clockwise in a beautiful crystal blue ball that fits nicely in the palm of your hand. Hold your hand on the chakra until you can see it as healthy. Keeping one hand on the throat chakra, place the other on your sixth chakra. Feel the energy moving upward between your hands. Feel the connection between the two chakras. Once you feel this healthy movement upward, you are ready to balance the sixth chakra.

Third Eye Chakra

Place both hands on your third eye. Feel the energy in your sixth chakra. Notice any differences in the fluctuations of the energy. Does it flow freely? Picture the chakra in your third eye as you connect with the energy. Notice its movement. Is it spinning? Is it moving in a clockwise or counterclockwise direction? What is the color? Is it a beautiful, deep indigo? Is it light blue or perhaps a shade of blue mixed with any other color? Notice the chakra's shape. Is it round or oval-shaped? Observe the chakra size. Would it fit nicely in your palm? It is the size of a grapefruit? Is it the size of a peanut?

If you notice anything out of the ordinary, ask your body why there is an imbalance. What is it about? Imagine the chakra healthy, spinning clockwise in a beautiful indigo ball that fits nicely in the palm of your hand. Hold your hand on the chakra until you can see it as healthy. Keeping one hand on the third eye chakra, place the other on your seventh, at the top of your head, your crown chakra. Feel the energy moving upward between your hands. Feel the connection between the two chakras. Once you feel this healthy movement upward, you are ready to balance the seventh chakra

Crown Chakra

Place both hands on your crown or seventh chakra. Feel the energy in your seventh chakra. Notice any differences in the fluctuations of the energy. Does it flow freely? Picture the chakra with your third eye as you connect with the energy. Notice its movement. Is it spinning? Is it moving in a clockwise or counterclockwise direction? What is the chakra color? Is it white? Is it a shade of white blended with some other color? Notice the chakra shape. Is it round or oval-shaped? Observe the chakra size. Would it fit nicely in your palm? It is the size of a grapefruit? Is it the size of a peanut?

If you notice anything out of the ordinary, ask your body why there is an imbalance. What is it about? Imagine the chakra healthy, spinning clockwise in a angelic white ball of energy that fits perfectly in the palm of your hand. Hold your hand on the chakra until you can see it as healthy.

Keeping both hands on your crown chakra, send the energy from your head to your feet. Feel the energy bouncing in your body, aligning all your chakra points. Feel your chakras spinning in a healthy vibrant light. Enjoy the peace you have created within your body. Spend some time here relishing this perfect balance.

Once you're done, be sure to again picture your feet deeply rooted in the earth. Focus your attention on your root chakra at the base of your spine at the end of the pubic bone. You may place your hand over it if you would like. Feel the energy in this chakra pulsating and spinning in a clockwise direction. See its bright vibrant red color. It is full of life and healthy.

Now see a bright red cord from this energy point on your body. Envision it flowing down to the center of the earth. Connect this cord to the deep red core of the planet. Feel the earth's magnetic current pulling your energy down. Feel all the energy in your head being pulled down; it flows through your neck and into your chest. Feel the energy pulled down to the lungs and through the digestive track as the energy flows down to the root chakra the pull is strong. The energy continues down your legs, through your feet. You are deeply connected to the earth. You are grounded in the earth's energy, and you are fully present. Sit for a moment and really feel the strength of this connection as it roots you in your life. Now you can release the cord connecting your root chakra to the earth's core. See it falling to the center of the earth and watch it be absorbed.

When you are ready, open your eyes. May your day be filled with light and love, and may you feel deeply connected to everyone and everything around you.

SIXTEEN

Psychic Senses

Now that you've worked on meditation and balancing your chakras, you're ready to begin working with your psychic senses. As mentioned earlier in this book, we use our psychic senses to communicate with spirits. This chapter of exercises helps you develop your psychic senses. You may find that some exercises are easier than others. This may happen because one sense is stronger than another for you. Developing psychic abilities takes time and practice, but it is innate for all of us.

Clairsentience

Clairsentience is the ability that allows us to perceive energy through feeling. It is governed by the sacral chakra, which is located two inches below the navel. This ability allows us to feel others' emotions and experiences. In my practice of helping people expand their psychic abilities, clairsentience is often the first developed ability. It often precedes third-eye (clairvoyant) development.

I think because clairsentience relies on the physical body to convey energy and information, people often dismiss it as a psychic sense. I refer to as it "the overlooked psychic ability." People often tell me that they *feel* the energy of a loved one. They'll say, "I feel my mother around me sometimes." When I ask them to further describe what they feel, they say things like "it feels loving" or "it feels warm and comforting to me." These people are using their clairsentient abilities to perceive the spirit energy around them.

Highly clairsentient people are also known as empaths. This level of ability can be an issue for some people if they don't know how to manage it. Without psychic shielding, empaths can take in too much energy and have difficulty distinguishing between their own feelings and what they're feeling from others. In addition, they can become overwhelmed in crowded situations. They may generally appear overly emotional from taking in too much energy. Learning to balance the sacral chakra and shielding one's own energy can manage all of these issues.

Hand-Holding Exercise

What you will need for this and the next exercise, Across from Partner:

- Your mind in a clear, relaxed state

- Two friends/family members in close physical proximity to you

• A journal and writing instrument

1. Sit across from your partner, and cup your partner's left hand with both of your hands.

2. Close your eyes, and connect with your partner's energy.

3. Take a mental note of any information you feel. This may include emotions and experiences.

4. Write down notes of what you encounter.

5. Share your finding with your partner.

6. Repeat the exercise, reversing roles.

Across from Partner Exercise (Clairsentience)

1. Sit in a chair facing a new partner. Set your chair about two feet away from your partner's chair.

2. Close your eyes, and place your hand over your sacral chakra point, just below your navel.

3. Feel the chakra balance and spin in a circular motion. Observe the bright orange color.

4. Focus your energy on your sacral chakra. Use it to feel the emotions and energy of your partner.

5. Write down notes of what you encounter.

6. Share your findings with your partner.

7. Repeat the exercise with a different partner.

Clairvoyance

Clairvoyance is the psychic sense that allows us to see things clearly without the use of physical eyes. It uses the third eye chakra located in the center of the forehead. With this sense, we can perceive physical images of people, places, and events. Mediums who have developed their sight can see spirits using their physical eyes as well as their third eyes. The following activity helps you develop your clairvoyant sense.

Color Exercise

What you will need for this exercise:

- Your mind in a clear, relaxed state

- A friend/family member in the same room as you

This is one of my son's favorite exercises. I would use it to entertain him on long car rides or while waiting for a seat in a restaurant. One person is the "thinker" and the other person is the "guesser." The thinker has to choose a color. The guesser has to try to figure out which color the thinker has selected. The thinker has to say, "I'm thinking of a color." This is the last verbal communication from the thinker until the color is guessed. Right after saying this statement, the thinker must concentrate on the color and see it (using the third eye) over and over again in his/her mind. For example, if the color selected is green, the thinker must contemplate the image of green.

The guesser must concentrate and try to clear his/her head of any thoughts and images not pertaining to the color.

The guesser must try to use her third eye to visualize the color the thinker has chosen. The guesser says different colors and the thinker nods if the guesser is correct or moves his head from side to side if the guesser is incorrect. You will notice progress, as you're able to identify the thinker's color in fewer guesses than when you first started the exercise.

You may also move from primary colors to more complex ones like chartreuse, tangerine, etc. Once you have tried it a few times, switch roles. Some people may find that one role is easier than the other. In time, you can be a master at both.

Clairaudience

Clairaudience helps us to hear information without the use of physical ears. We hear thoughts of others, experiences, or spirit communication conveyed nonverbally. This ability is also referred to as mental telepathy, which is the communication of information through thoughts. Psychically, we have this ability to use regularly with friends and family.

At any point in your life, have you struggled with something and you heard the answer in your mind? This could have been someone in spirit form helping you with the answer. Passed-on loved ones and friends often use clairaudience to relay messages and information to us particularly when we struggle in our daily lives.

Number Exercise

What you will need for this exercise:

- Your mind in a clear, relaxed state
- A friend/family member in close physical proximity to you

This is another one of my son's favorites, and we play it when we run out of colors in the previous game of guessing colors. This game uses a thinker and guesser as well. The main difference between this exercise and the color exercise is that the former yields an essentially infinite number of possibilities and the game can go on for a long time. At first you may want to use single digits, one through five. When you are more comfortable, increase the range to one through ten.

The thinker contemplates a number and keeps saying it over and over internally. The difference between this exercise and the clairvoyance one is that instead of thinking of a color and visualizing it, the thinker sends thoughts of the word he has selected. The guesser once again clears the mind of all thoughts except those involving the numbers. As before, the guesser tries to intercept the thinker's thought process and perceive the number's word.

The goal of this exercise is to get you to rely on mind communication. As the thinker, you're sending thoughts with your mind rather than communicating verbally. As the guesser, you're trying to receive the thoughts of the thinker.

It takes some practice, but it's also great fun. I highly recommend it for children; it's an exciting and mentally stimulating way to keep them entertained.

Telepathic Communication

Now that you've worked on using your clairaudience with someone in the same room as you, try working with someone at a greater distance from you. Through telepathic communication, we can transmit our thoughts, feelings, and emotions. We can also receive information telepathically. We use our clairaudient psychic skill to enable this type of communication.

Once you enable your mind as a communication tool, you'll find its ability is limitless. Geographic boundaries no longer exist. Have you ever thought of a friend and that day or the next day, they call you out of the blue? Perhaps they were able to mentally perceive your thinking of them. The easiest way to try telepathic communication is with another living person. Once you have mastered telepathic communication with the living, you can move on to communicating nonverbally with spirits.

Basic Telepathic Call Exercise
What you will need for this exercise:

- Your mind in a clear, relaxed state

- A friend/family member in close proximity
  to your home

• Journal and writing instrument

• A physical telephone

I recommend trying this with someone in close physical proximity but not in the same house, building, or location as you. You may want to try it with a close neighbor or friend. Choose someone you feel connected to because the communication will be easier for you. You can sit anywhere you feel comfortable.

1. Using your mind, call out to that person with your thoughts and ask them to call you.

2. Ask them three times with your mind, e.g., "Jane Doe—please physically call me on the telephone."

3. Write down the date and time you called out to your friend or family member.

4. If a day goes by and you have not received your call, repeat the exercise, asking your friend three times with your mind.

5. Again, write the date and time you called out to your friend.

6. Repeat this pattern until you receive your call.

7. Write down the date and time you received your call.

8. Using your journal, determine how long it took for you to receive your call from your friend.

9. Try the exercise again using a different person.
   See if you have made progress (i.e., less time
   passing) since the first time you tried the exercise.

If you do the exercise a few times with a few different people, see if there is a correlation between the closeness of your relationship with that person and the length
of time it takes to complete the exercise. You may find
that you have a stronger telepathic communication with
people closest to you—and they do not have to be family
members. You may find that the exercise is easier with
your closest friends because you share a strong bond.

SEVENTEEN

Contacting
Your Guides

All of us have spirit guides, which are spirits assigned to us in this lifetime to help navigate the process of life on earth. Our guides are chosen before we incarnate. All spirit guides share one common goal—to aid the living person in fulfilling his/her life purpose. Aside from that fact, there are other variables that come into play based on the individual to whom the guides are assigned.

Many people have questions about spirits guides, and there aren't any answers that apply across the board. The specifics involving spirit guides are unique to the individual on earth and his/her life purpose. Spirit guides may have been past family members, friends, or someone without an earthly connection to us. All spirit guides were once in physical form at some point. They can be the souls of children or adults. Some people have one or two guides, while others may have several of them. Some guides may be with you for only a short time to help you through a certain experience, while others may be with you for your whole physical life. Our guides are by our sides daily and can be of great assistance if we decide to engage them.

Meeting Your Guides Exercise

What you will need for this exercise:

- Your mind

- A quiet place

  1. Sit comfortably in a chair or reclined position.

  2. Close your eyes and take a few deep, calming breaths.

  3. Relax your thoughts. Let them flow and in and out of your mind. Don't pay attention to them or follow them.

  4. Using your mind's eye, imagine a big blue bubble encompassing you safely.

  5. Picture yourself completely protected in this cooling blue energy. Feel the security and comfort of the bubble.

6. Focus once again on relaxing the mind and body. Breathe in to the count of three and out to the count of three. Feel every cell of your body relaxing with each exhale. Sit for a moment and enjoy this peaceful state you have created for yourself.

7. Now that you are totally relaxed yet in an alert state, focus on your third eye. Pay attention to any colors or images you see. Do not be discouraged if you don't see any spirits; not everyone will see them. It really depends on how open your third eye is at the time. It is just as valid to feel and hear information connected to your guides. Ask your guides to come forward from the brilliant white light.

8. Once you sense that your guides are present, ask a question. When you first reach out to them, you may only want to ask one or two questions so you can work on sending and receiving information telepathically with your guides. You can ask them any one of the following:

   a. What is your name?

   b. Can you come into focus so I can see you?

   c. How are you connected to me?

   d. Is there a specific purpose for which you are providing guidance?

9. Imagine a long red cord from your root chakra (just below the pubic bone) to the center of the earth. Feel all of your energy being pulled to the center of the earth. Notice the sense of comfort and stability as you connect. Once you feel this deep connection, imagine the cord releasing from your root chakra, falling to the center of the earth.

10. Send your bubble back up to the sky and thank the universe for this experience.

Always end a communication session with your guides by thanking them for all the work they do to help you achieve your life goals.

You may hear a response in your thoughts, or you may see images in your third eye that answer your question. You may also feel the information and experiences. You will receive information in whichever one of your extra-sensory faculties is most attuned.

When you are done communicating with your guides, write down any notes on information, images, emotions, or experiences relayed in the session. Once you have done this, you are ready to ground yourself. You can ground your energy in many different ways. The method listed here is only one example of a quick grounding visualization.

After you've made initial contact with your guides, try to set a time monthly or even weekly to regularly connect with them. This time can be beneficial not only for connecting with your guides but also for connecting with your soul. Your guides will help you gain insight and direction. In addition, the more you work on communicating with them, the easier it is to engage with them. Perhaps you will begin by meditating to connect with them, and maybe as time goes on, you'll be able to communicate regularly by simply thinking of them, sending and receiving thoughts.

Shielding Your Energy

Once you know how to engage your guides, you need to learn to shield your energy on a regular basis. When we open ourselves to spirit communication, we need to block out unwanted energy. We do this by soliciting the help of our guides and also by psychically shielding our energies.

I generally use visualization shielding methods, but there are also physical methods that may include wearing or carrying a psychic shielding stone. Lapis lazuli is a beautiful blue semiprecious stone. One of its metaphysical properties includes subverting psychic attack.

My mother gave me a lapis and gold necklace when I was seventeen. Though I didn't wear it much, I always kept it in the jewelry box in my bedroom. As I began opening to mediumship, I decided one day to wear the necklace and love it. I did not know of its metaphysical properties at the time, but I felt drawn to wearing it. Even now, if I change my jewelry to go out to dinner or an event, I replace the lapis necklace around my neck when I return.

Other psychic shielding stones include amethyst, clear quartz, ruby, and black tourmaline, to name a few. Wearing one of these stones in a piece of jewelry transmits a vibration that helps shield your energy. If you do not have the stone set in jewelry, you may also carry a rough or small tumbled stone in a pocket. Stones of this sort can be found in metaphysical and New Age stores.

People may also use religious jewelry or amulets for psychic shielding depending on their belief systems. Sometimes people wear crosses or dove necklaces, charms with relics of saints, medicine bags with herbs and other objects, pentagrams, and Star of David jewelry. All these objects are symbols of spirituality and give people a sense of spiritual protection. In addition to these objects, however, I still favor some type of visualization method when communicating with spirits. I would especially recommend adding a visualization technique when you are trying to communicate with a loved one or friend.

Here is a list of some visualization exercises I recommend for energy shielding. Use whichever one is most comfortable for you.

Psychic Shielding Exercises

Bubble Technique

1. Picture a colored bubble descending from the sky.

2. Make the bubble whatever color you wish.
   See the bubble encasing you completely. Feel
   the warm, loving energy flowing throughout
   the bubble.

3. Allow this protective energy to permeate every cell of your body.

4. Press your legs and hands outwards, touching the wall of the bubble.

5. Know that you are safe and totally protected.

Shower of Light (my favorite)

1. Using your mind, envision showers of light in whatever color you wish falling gently from above, cascading over you.

2. Allow this brilliant rain of light to fall and illuminate all aspects of your being.

3. See it brightly coloring you inside and out.

4. Watch as the light pools around your feet in beautiful colored puddles.

5. Feel the sense of protection this light carries in it.

6. Know that you are loved and safe.

Tunneling Light

1. Imagine a magnificent tunnel of light in your color of choice descending from the heavens, down to your head.

2. As it pours over you, the tunnel envelopes your entire body with an illuminating brilliance. Watch it funnel from your head down to your toes and back up to your head.

3. Observe its luminosity moving within your body.

4. Once it has filled you, see it spinning around you encasing you in a tornado of light.

5. Feel the swiftly moving tunnel as it securely wraps you in a blanket of protection.

6. Know that you are safe and secure in this light.

7. Watch as the tunnel ascends back up to the sky and dissipates in the clouds.

Grounding Our Energies

Before we go over a few methods of grounding, let us first discuss the meaning of the term. Often people say things like, "my spouse keeps me grounded" or "my job keeps me grounded." They are using the term "grounded" to mean focused or centered. When we talk about grounding our energy, we mean to pull the energy close to the earth. The energetic meaning is a little different from the general meaning. On the energetic level, we are focusing our minds, souls, and bodies. We are uniting our complete selves and keeping them on earth.

When we communicate with spirit, we raise our vibrations to a higher level. We use the top three chakras for clairaudience, clairvoyance, and clairsentience. When we are through with the communication, we need to adapt our souls to once again be connected to our bodies and close to the earth. We need to pull our energy down through the lower chakras. Sometimes a person may feel light-headed or a little scattered after a communication session. These sensations are common as your soul/mind/body reconnect. Grounding solidifies the connection and also keeps you centered.

After all spirit communication sessions, it is imperative to ground your energy. You can accomplish this task by one of several ways listed below:

1. Cord from Root Chakra

Imagine a red cord from your root chakra(just below your navel) to the center of the earth. Place your hand over the root chakra, and feel your connection with the earth.

2. Roots from Earth

Imagine roots growing up from your feet through your legs, pulling your energy close to the ground. When you feel centered, see the roots going back into the earth.

3. Grounding Stone

Hold a piece of hematite (or another grounding stone like obsidian) in your left hand and feel your energy pull downwards. Envision all your energy pulling downward to the center of the earth.

4. Physical Method 1

Walk outside in bare feet and connect with the earth.

5. Physical Method 2

Drink a full glass of water.

6. Physical Method 3

Eat a piece of fresh fruit or a fresh vegetable.

EIGHTEEN

Communicating with Passed-on Loved Ones

Once you have mastered the telepathic communication exercise, know how to engage your guides, and understand energy shielding, you're ready to communicate with your passed-on loved ones. Initially, the information will come through to you in your strongest psychic sense, whichever one is most comfortable and natural. You may feel, hear, see, smell, or taste information from your loved one or friend. As you become more proficient, information may come through more than one sense.

When we first try to communicate with our loved ones, we can ask them to send us a sign. The sign or symbol can be anything in the physical world like an animal, sound, smell, or object. We should ask them for something that holds specific meaning for us. This is an important aspect because without the sign having specific meaning, we might dismiss it. You may ask a loved one to send a blue butterfly or a blue jay. You may also ask them to send a familiar scent like that of your favorite flower or perhaps a perfume the person wore. Sometimes a song has specific meaning, so people like to ask for it as a sign. If they hear it right after they've requested it, they know they've received the sign.

Sometimes people aren't comfortable asking for physical signs, but they still want confirmation that their loved ones are okay on the other side. In this situation, they may want to ask for a dream visit from a loved one. When we dream, we're in a relaxed state and most of our conscious defense mechanisms are down, so we're more open to receiving information from a loved one.

The main difference between a dream visit and ordinary dream is that when someone wakes from a dream visit, they actually feel like their loved one was there with them. The person can recall the dream details with vivid clarity and can relay the emotions associated with the experience. Often when we wake from our dreams the details are hazy; we recall only bits and pieces. In a dream visit, we remember all details—even the most minor ones—which may include the words spoken or sounds hear, actions conveyed, the setting, emotions felt, and any scents.

Most people want to know that their crossed-over loved ones are at peace. Asking for signs and dream visits are two ways for our family members and loved ones to come through and validate that they are okay and their souls do indeed live on in the afterlife. We don't need any special skills for these methods; we just need open minds.

Asking for a Sign Exercise

What you will need for this exercise:

- Your mind in a clear, relaxed state

- A peaceful environment

Before we try to communicate with spirits, let us remember the two basic steps:

1. Shield our energy

2. Call in our guides

These steps are necessary to ensure we connect with the highest vibrational energy and that we are only attracting the spirits of those with whom we wish to communicate. Once you have completed these steps, you are ready to begin.

1. Using your mind, call out to your loved one using a birth name and birth date.

2. If you do not have this specific information, you may also think of the person.

3. Fill your head with warm memories; replay them over and over in your mind.

4. Once again, call out to the person with your mind by thinking of their name three times.

5. Ask the person to send you a validating sign.

6. Send the person a thought of the specific sign you want to see, feel, hear, smell, or taste. You can choose an image, or something physical like a bird or animal, or a song.

7. Write down the date you asked for a sign.

8. When you get your sign, write down the date.

9. Take note of how long it took for the person to send you the sign.

Once you receive your sign (it could take a day or several days), send a thought of thanks and love to your loved one. Invite the person to send a sign or message any time they need to, and know that the person comes to you with more love and support than you can ever imagine. Thank God for the connection you have to your loved ones because without the divine intervention, it would not exist.

An Additional Note About Signs from Spirits

Sometimes spirits of loved ones send signs or symbols randomly, although they are usually sent in response to some request we have. Perhaps during a time of distress we mentally or verbally called out to them, asking for a sign. When we receive our signs, they are validations that our requests have been heard.

But often we're tuned out when there are spirits around trying to help us. These spirits may have to be a little more active in presenting their signs to us. Remember that spirits are energy forms without bodies, yet they are trying to communicate with humans, which are physically very dense matter (I don't mean that in a sarcastic way!) that generally use their bodies and its five senses to perceive information. As a result, spirits have to use signs that cater to our senses of sight, hearing, smell, taste, and touch.

Let us first address the vibrational issue of spirits. Most spirits vibrate at a higher frequency than humans, so in order to communicate with us, they need to slow down their vibrations. This can take some practice. In addition, spirits are forms comprised of electromagnetic energy, the same type of energy field in our electrical and radio waves. As a result, when spirits are around, their energy fields disrupt those fields, creating disturbances in the reception. These disturbances may manifest in flickering of lights, sound not working on the television, and radio stations losing their frequencies. All of these are little ways to let us know that spirits are around us.

Other times, spirits may need to resort to more drastic signs to get our attention. Perhaps we are heavy with grief, feeling depressed, or maybe even going in the wrong direction in life. You may hear a large crash and search all over to find nothing out of place. Spirits can and will move things. It takes a lot of energy for them to perform these acts, so it is not a regular occurrence unless they really need to get someone's attention. Things can fly off shelves, objects might be moved, and furniture may be rearranged. Spirits that resort to this drastic type of activity are not always there to help us. In fact, they often need our help.

I have a friend who called me to clear her apartment because every time she came home from work, the furniture was rearranged. Upon visiting the apartment, I found the culprit was a woman who had lived there and passed on. Due to her sudden passing, she remained in a somewhat confused state, thinking the place was still her home. She could not understand why my friend was there. After explaining the situation to the confused spirit, I helped her cross, and the apartment returned to normal.

There are several reasons spirits send us signs. We need to be open and interpret them as necessary. They could be sending us a sign to aid us, or they might send a sign to elicit help from us for someone else. When we learn about spirit signs and how to interpret them, the spirit realm and Earth plane can coexist peacefully for everyone's benefit.

Asking for a Dream Visit Exercise
What you will need for this exercise:

- Your mind in a relaxed state

- A quiet environment

Before we try to communicate with spirits, we *must* shield our energy and call in our guides.

1. Using your mind, call out to your loved one using the person's birth name and birth date.

2. If you do not have this specific information, you may also think of the person.

3. Fill your head with warm memories about the person and replay them over and over in your mind.

4. Once again, call out to the person with your mind by thinking of their name three times.

5. Ask the person to visit you in a dream.

6. Write down the initial date that you asked for your dream visit. You can send your loved one a mental request each night before bed.

7. When you get your dream visit, write down the date.

8. Take note of how long it took for the person to send you the dream visit.

Once you receive your dream visit (it could take a day or several days), send your loved one loving thoughts of gratitude. Leave the door of communication open for them to visit in a dream state at any time. Thank God for the divine spiritual connection you have with your loved ones.

Communicating with Spirits of Children

The loss of a child can be an incredibly difficult time for any parent, whether the child passes as an infant or an adult. I have met with many parents who have lost children, and although the specifics of each experience are different, they all share a couple common feelings such as guilt and anger. As loving parents we feel responsible for children, even after physical passings. Many parents wonder who will look after their children and who will help their souls. What parents may not realize is that God has planned for these passings and all of the logistics are coordinated. There are always souls of passed-on family and friends on the other side to cross children—someone will look after them; they're never alone. They meet with a soul group of other souls with a shared mission, and they work together on the other side.

Often, parents feel like they're being punished or singled out by God when their children pass. I have heard parents ask, "Why did God take my child? What did I do wrong?" This anger can cause parents to lose their faith. They have done nothing wrong, however—God needs the child's soul on the other side for a very specific purpose.

I have a friend who lost a daughter in a car crash; she was just twenty-one years of age. My friend learned to communicate with her daughter through symbols and dreams. Whenever she saw the symbol, she knew her daughter was around. When her husband was ill, she asked her daughter to send the symbol to verify that she was helping the father. A day later, my friend got her symbol.

An acquaintance of mine asked me to reach out to her brother, who had also passed in a car accident. Ironically, as I spoke with the brother, my friend's daughter came through. She explained how she helped this man cross over, though she had no relationship to him. She told me that on the other side, she worked with sudden accident victims. She sent them "where they needed to go," as she put it. Apparently, sometimes a sudden accident can be jarring for a soul, causing confusion. My friend's daughter and others like her work to get these souls in the right area so they can move on. At the time of her daughter's passing, my friend had no idea why God had taken her child. After her visit with me, my friend not only understood why God her taken her child but also why she left the earth through a car accident. Her daughter's passing was and still is directly related to her job on the other side.

Parents share an eternal loving bond with their children that supersedes physical death. When parents understand that the souls of their children live on, they can open to a continued spiritual relationship with them. As parents let go of grief, they will find their children lovingly waiting for them to engage in a different sort of relationship—one that involves signs, dreams, thoughts, and symbols. When children cross over, we need to abandon hopes of physical relationships with them and embrace the concept of an everlasting spiritual relationships.

Communication with Victims
Who Pass Suddenly

The sudden passing of a loved one can jolt us whether it occurs by accident or an unexpected physical condition. When our loved ones exit abruptly, we're left with many loose ends that long for closure. We may feel as though the loved one was ripped away from us; there were likely things we wanted to do together or say. We are left with raw emotions and unanswered questions. Often, we miss the opportunity to say goodbye or perhaps "I love you" one last time.

My maternal grandfather, Pops, passed suddenly. Our relationship had been fractured a bit when he remarried about five years before his passing. His new wife didn't care much for keeping a relationship with his children or grandchildren. As a result, visits were less frequent and we lost our closeness. My son only met him a few times as a young baby. What had once been a relationship of frequent visiting had changed into a series of monthly phone calls (on my part) and visits once a quarter, even though he moved to New Jersey and lived just twenty minutes from us.

Late one evening, my mother got a call saying Pops had been rushed to the hospital with a brain aneurysm and was on life support. Unbeknownst to the rest of the family, she raced to be by his side and stayed for several hours. My mother left the hospital around 2:00 am to get a little bit of sleep. She drove back to the hospital around 7:30 am once again to say a final goodbye. What she didn't know was that

Pops's new wife had already ordered him off the life support earlier that morning and my mother missed him in transit.

Shortly after my mother left the house, my father received a call from the neurologist saying that Pops's condition had worsened and the family needed to make a decision. Apparently, the doctor was unaware of the wife's order to take him off life support. My father urged the doctor to keep him on life support until we arrived. Then my father called me and said we should go up to the hospital to say goodbye.

As I hung up the phone, tears streamed down my cheeks. I felt Pops right there next to me, his energy vibrating in warm, golden glow.

"You know it didn't have to be like this," I said tearfully. He apologized for the way he had hurt the family and said he loved all of us. He wanted to convey his love before he left. I told him that I loved him, and then he was gone.

When my father arrived to take me to the hospital, I told him about the visit and that I knew Pops had already died. He insisted that it was some type of mistake because the hospital was waiting for us to arrive. I knew my father was wrong; Pops had already left the Earth plane. Ironically, when we got to the hospital, we found my youngest brother, Kyle, sitting on the floor outside the room. His head hung low and tears glistened in his eyes. He had been there for a couple of hours. He had decided to venture to the hospital early that morning, having a feeling something was drastically wrong with Pops. He walked into the room right after they pulled Pops off life support and found a Catholic priest giving him the sacrament of Anointing of the Sick—a final blessing and forgiveness for those who are ill.

When my father and I entered the room, we knew Pops had been gone for a while. The place felt lifeless, his cold body propped up by bed pillows and stark white sheets accenting his pale grayish skin. My mother sat sobbing in a chair. I was grateful he came to visit me right after he died because the room's empty despair disturbed me. I later shared the information he communicated with the other family members, hoping it would soothe the sting of his abrupt passing.

Often our family members arrive by our sides during sudden passings but we aren't always aware of these visits. They come to say goodbye and wish us love before they cross over. If by chance we miss this comforting visit, there is something we can do to ease our pain and communicate those final words and thoughts to our loved ones. We can write a simple letter and read it out loud. They'll hear every word, and in time we'll get some type of validation from them.

Writing a Letter to a Victim Who Suddenly Passed
What you will need for this exercise:

- Your mind in a relaxed state

- A quiet environment

- Pen or pencil and paper

Before we try to communicate with spirits, we *must* shield our energy and call in our guides.

1. Sit in a quite place with your piece of paper and pen or pencil.

2. Allow yourself to think of a mental picture of your loved one.

3. Write down everything you want to share, and be sure to include any unanswered questions if you have any.

4. Ask your loved one to send responses in whatever method is most acceptable to you.

5. Sit for a moment and silently read the letter. Make sure you have included everything you want to say.

6. When you're ready, read the letter aloud. Take as much time as you need.

7. Spend a moment quietly reflecting on this experience.

8. Using your mind, ask you loved one to send you a response at some point in whichever method is most acceptable to you: through a dream, with a symbol or sign, or through your thoughts.

9. Send them thoughts of love and gratitude.

How We Can Help Suicide Victims

The subject of suicide comes up in my mediumship work. It's important to make the distinction between suicide and a death in which someone overdosed on a substance. Accidental overdose deaths are not necessarily suicides. The distinction between the two is in the intention of the person at the time of physical death. In the case of suicide, one consciously decides to take his or her life.

My understanding of what happens to a soul following a suicide is based on experience. People commit suicide for a variety of reasons, but most involve deep-seated emotions such as anger, confusion, depression, and loneliness—just to list a few. Often, after their passings, suicide victims remain in this emotional state until someone reaches out to them.

In Hinduism, there's a Sanskrit word, *dharma*, and one of its meanings can be translated into "life purpose." When one doesn't know or follow the dharma, disease can manifest. Although I'm Catholic, I think the concept of life purpose is universal. We're all here for very specific purposes. When we take our own lives, our purposes on Earth remain unfulfilled. In my experience with suicide victims, beyond the deep-seated emotions is often a disconnect in the person's life purpose.

Suicide victims cannot speak for themselves and aren't readily available to communicate with the living. Their souls require deep healing. The ability for communication with their living loved ones and friends often comes in the process of healing.

Suicide is an act shrouded in darkness and lower vibrational energy. Family members can reach out to these victims through prayer, loving thoughts, or by verbally calling out to them and sending them into the light. Once someone reaches out and helps guides them into the light, the soul can begin healing. In my experience, suicide victims go to a special place on the other side. It's a place of compassionate love and they're there for as long as they need healing. Some souls choose not to heal. They reject their guides and literally roam in darkness. But God is benevolent, and the door to healing is always open, whenever they're ready to walk through it.

Helping Victims of Suicide Exercise
What you will need for this exercise:

- Your mind in a relaxed state

- A quiet environment

Before we try to help suicide victims, we need to shield our energy and call in our guides. You *cannot* skip these two steps. Suicide is a dark act covered in darkness, and you will need to block out any impressions associated with that energy. You are only sending help to your loved one.

1. Picture yourself in a brightly colored bubble or tunnel yourself in light.

2. Next, call in your guides and ask them to be with you for guidance and protection.

3. Using your mind recall a mental image of the person you are trying to reach.

4. Call the person's name.

5. Tell the soul to get up and step into the light.

6. Assure the person that everything is okay and the person will be healed.

7. Tell the soul that other loved ones are waiting for them in the light.

Thank your guides for helping you with this experience and thank the universe for the ability to help others. When we help others, we grow closer to each other and God; we're all connected—part of the whole. If you know any people touched by suicide, send them loving thoughts and healing. Pray for their emotional scars to heal. Suicide leaves people in darkness and sadness. Sending light can help the healing process for everyone touched by the experience.

Pets and the Afterlife

Of course, as a medium, I believe pets have souls and can send signs, symbols and dream visits from the afterlife just like humans. Sometimes we need to hear true stories to remind us that everything is possible including the compassion of our pets in the afterlife.

As you already know from previous chapters in this book, our first pet was a crazy chocolate Labrador Retriever named Timber who had a boxy head and amber puppy eyes that drooped when he grew tired. He melted my heart the moment I met him. His penchant for baked goods included all homemade cakes and cookies and a special fondness for Dunkin Donuts; I think he recognized the box or perhaps the smell. Whenever someone brought a box of those sugary treats into our home, Timber stalked them like a shark tracing a chum slick. He always managed to steal one or two even though it meant he'd be banished to the backyard for an hour or so—a small price to pay for such a rare delicacy to the canine palate.

I wish I could say he was a good boy, but he was actually the antithesis. He chewed a kitchen set and many other things in his puppyhood. He improved slightly as he matured but always managed to do "bad boy" things like stick his head in the kitchen trash can and steal food. Though he ate all the candy canes and chewed at least four Christmas tree ornaments each year, we loved him for being Timber—our unique dog who would sleep in the bathtub during thunderstorms.

At the young age of eleven, he developed an aggressive form of facial cancer. I immediately began looking for natural ways to help him. I found a holistic veterinarian that treated him with herbs rather than chemotherapy and radiation. At the time, I was studying my Reiki Master level certification. I gave him Reiki every day and he seemed happy and healthy, but his cancer grew. I continued to seek alternative therapies for him including aromatherapy, diet changes, and lymphatic massage. I realized that Timber's cancer had an important effect on me; it spurred my development as a healer. I recognized that our relationship was much more than pet and owner—there was a spiritual connection between us.

The day Timber died, we drove him to the veterinarian knowing he wouldn't be coming home with us. My heart ached as I called out to Nanny to help him cross. As he inhaled his last breath, I saw her standing across from me, and I knew he was in good hands. During the tearful drive home from that night, I sent him a mental message to give me a sign when he crossed. I asked for a blue butterfly. Later that same night, I woke and glanced in the hallway to find him standing there. His coat glistened brilliantly and his tail wagged happily from left to right. I felt tears on my face, but perhaps they were tears of joy knowing he was okay. When I wiped my tears, he vanished from my sight.

The following morning, we took our son and other two Labradors to the cranberry bog for our Saturday walk. I missed Timber's mischievous energy. Though the brisk morning air nipped our skin as usual and the hawks routinely weaved through the trees, the walk felt foreign and strange without Shane chasing Timber out of the bog. My eyes watered when we crossed the bridge over the tea-colored creek. Timber loved swimming in it and I missed watching him thrash about in the water. Just then, the most stunning bright blue butterfly fluttered around my face for a few moments, as Shane and I gazed in amazement. I've never seen another blue butterfly. I accepted this as a special gift of validation from Timber, and I sent him thoughts of gratitude not only for the sign but also for sharing a remarkable part of my life.

The souls of pets live on in the afterlife. They're able to send us signs and symbols and visit us in dreams just like other spirits. They remain connected to us and know when we need assistance. Like all our loved ones is spirit form, they are only a thought away from us.

NINETEEN

Space Clearing

After we communicate with spirits on any level, we want to clear the space of any residual energy. There are several methods for space clearing. Like the energy protection methods, I favor visualization techniques. But there are other physical methods you can employ. Smudging is a technique mentioned earlier in this book. It involves using the smoke of a smoldering dried herb bundle to cleanse and clear the energy in a space. Some people use essential oils to clear space, while others burn white candles in each room. People may also use salt or cups of water in each room as well as fresh flowers and herbs.

One of my favorite methods of space clearing involves tunneling light. It's a method used to clear one's own energy as well as environmental energy and only takes a couple of minutes to complete.

Space Clearing Exercise

What you will need for this exercise:

- Your mind in a relaxed state

- A quiet environment

1. Close your eyes and relax.

2. In your mind, select a color that appeals to you; it can be any color. I usually use gold.

3. Imagine a tunnel of golden (or whatever color you chose) light running from the heavens down to your head, through your body, and coming out of your feet.

4. Once the energy reaches your feet, see it coming back to your feet, funneling back up through your body to your head. When it reaches your head, the process gets repeated.

5. As your body fills with the golden light, see each cell illuminate. Feel the warmth fill your entire being.

6. Once you have filled your body with this light, start with a section of your home. Imagine a tunnel of this golden light funneling in a clockwise direction through a room in your house.

7. While it funnels and spins around, see it touch everything in the room as it casts an aura throughout.

8. As it finishes one room, see it move on to the next one—a tornado of healing light.

9. Picture this tunnel moving through all rooms in the house, including under the house and in any attic space.

10. Once the tunnel has cleared each room, picture it growing larger, engulfing the entire house.

11. As it bathes the house in a funnel of light, see it growing and spinning faster.

12. See any unwanted energy being pulled from the home, and out the tunnel and sent up to the angelic realm.

13. Open your eyes, close the tunnel down, and enjoy the peace you have created.

Cutting Energetic Cords

Cord cutting is a necessary task that should be completed daily. We connect our energy to others every day through our thoughts, actions, and experiences—sometimes even unintentionally. When we worry about a sick friend, we create an energetic cord between us. We create cords in all of our relationships. We can also form cords to places like a home or our jobs. But when we fail to cut cords, we create energetic drains that can affect us physically, emotionally, mentally, and spiritually.

Before we get into the cord cutting exercise, I would like to share a story in which I learned about cord cutting the hard way. A family member was in a nearby hospital about ten miles from my home. When I visited the hospital, I noticed it was a haven for lost and confused energy. At hospitals, sometimes people die and kind of stick around because they're not sure what happened or where to go. Their guides may direct these souls, but they sometimes resist crossing over because of earthly attachments.

As I left the hospital, I thought of including it in my evening ritual of tunneling and clearing. So after I cleared the house that night, I envisioned the hospital. I pictured a large tunnel of light going through each floor and clearing the space. Then I pictured it engulfing the entire hospital and all energies connected to it were funneled through the top and up to the heavens.

About three nights later at 2:00 in the morning, the smoke alarm in the upstairs hallway blared (there was no smoke), waking the entire house. Shane took the batteries out, and when I walked into the hall, I saw a dark-haired, middle-aged man in a hospital gown. I asked him why he was there, and he said he wanted to get a message to his wife. He had passed of a heart attack at a construction site earlier that day and wanted me to tell his wife that he was okay. I crossed him and then everyone went back to bed.

The next night, the same thing happened. In the early morning, the smoke alarm in the upstairs hallway sounded. Shane took it down. This time, an elderly man with sparse gray hair stood in the hallway. He too, sported a lovely hospital gown baring his knobby knees. He didn't want to cross because he wanted to reach his family. When I asked him how he got to my house, he said he followed the light. I crossed him and then I sat on my bed and asked my guides, "What's with these people in hospital gowns?"

Although not much was said, I was shown an aerial view of my house and it was lit up in light. There was a bridge of white light connecting my house to the hospital.

"Still think it's a good idea to clear the hospital every night, kid?" my guide, John, asked. I thought I was doing something good. But by not cutting the cord between my house and the hospital each night, I had essentially created a wide-open bridge. I might as well have put a sign up that said "Spirits welcome here anytime." Even if they weren't looking for a medium, spirits were attracted to my house because of the light. I'm actually lucky that my house wasn't flooded with energy.

I thanked my guides for helping me and immediately cut the cord between my house and the hospital. Although we can connect our energy to other people or places, we need to cut the cords to avoid energetic issues.

Cord-Cutting Exercise

What you will need for this exercise:

- Your mind in a relaxed state

- A quiet environment

  1. Close your eyes and relax.

2. Envision your entire body in a tunnel of light.

3. Next, ask your guides to allow you to see all the cords connected to you; both those you consciously and unconsciously connect to.

4. Now envision all the cords being cut away from your tunnel of light.

5. Watch them fall to the center of the earth.

6. Take a moment and feel the jolt as you pull your energy back into your aura.

7. Feel how light you are without all those cords pulling you down, tying you to other people and places.

8. Enjoy the sense of weightlessness and peace you have created.

9. Thank your guides and the universe for aiding in this process.

Hopefully with a bit of practice and patience, you'll be on your way to communicating with your loved ones. I've given the exercises that cover all the basics, so practice each exercise several times until you've mastered it. Once you become proficient at an exercise, move on to the next one. I've included a recommended reading list of books by fellow Llewellyn authors for further reading along your developmental journey. May you always be held in the Light and eternally connected to your loved ones in spirit.

Recommended Reading List

Forever with You by Patrick Matthews

When Tomorrow Speaks to Me by Bridget Benson

Miraculous Moments by Elissa Al-Chokhachy

Growing Up Psychic by Michael Bodine

By Morning's Light by Ginny Brock

Spirit of Love by Jenny Crawford

The Happy Medium by Jodi Livon

Return to Intuition by Kathryn Harwig

My Life Across the Table by Karen Page

Magical Housekeeping by Tess Whitehurst

.

CPSIA information can be obtained
at www.ICGtesting.com
Printed in the USA
LVOW04s1701120816

500057LV00006B/10/P